THE INSTITUTIONAL DRIVE

CARL G. GUSTAVSON

The
Institutional Drive

OHIO UNIVERSITY PRESS

TO MY PARENTS
IMMIGRANTS TO WONDERLAND

CONTENTS

INTRODUCTION

During these past decades the United States of America has risen to an unparalleled pinnacle of physical power, while simultaneously the American mood of absolute faith in the success of our way of life has been increasingly tinged with bewilderment at its seeming rejection in many quarters elsewhere. Two world wars and the barbarism of fascism and communism have, at times, seemed to refute our basic presuppositions. We have been confronted by the organized challenge of the Communists, who interpret events in terms of a Right-Left dichotomy of politics wherein the path of progress bears steadily to the Left; in many parts of the world, and especially among youth, we are considered old-fashioned, doomed to perish as surely as the Old Regime crumbled before the rising bourgeoisie. While our military and economic strengths have thus far sufficed to maintain our world position, we have done rather less well on the battlefields of the mind with weapons of political philosophy often held outdated by the foreigner.

Our formal traditions still tend only to bespeak our original republicanism and our subsequent espousal of democracy, messages which once moved the world, but which in themselves are no longer enough. Ideals of an earlier day, expressing the certitudes of a more simple environment, often do not come to grips with the realities of the age, and need, consequently, to be amplified in the light of experiences and insights during the present century. Required, above all, is the recapture of a sense of progress, and of faith, by seeing beyond the momentary difficulties or setbacks to the longer sweep of history. We do have our own vision of progress, of a journey to a heavenly city on earth which has culminated for us in the arrival in our present land of overflowing abundance—our Wonderland. We were pioneers for the whole world in this adventure, and our example of what is possible has helped energize other peoples to undertake the same migration into a Wonderland built by science and technology.

Events of our century have shown, however, that this journey can also lead to disaster; the corollary of the promise of a Wonderland is the ever-present danger of the barbarism of a political Inferno. Americans possess the depths of experience out of the more recent past, our own migration on the frontiers of a technologically advancing commonwealth, to understand the reasons for these and kindred phenomena, to bring our political traditions into greater harmony with the realities of our times and thereby also resume an ideological leadership. If a more coherent political philosophy is needed in order to counter that of our antagonists, its ingredients are "in the air," readily perceptible to anyone who wishes to attempt to weave them into a unified expression of our destined role.

For instance, why are we so obtuse in our reluctance to incorporate our invaluable experiences with the modern association into our tradition? We persist in looking upon them as a divisive element, as morally unacceptable devices for obtaining special privileges, as a growth which somehow sullies the purity of our political institutions, while in actual practice we not only use them constantly, we have become inescapably dependent upon them for the very survival of democratic government. Neither formally a part of the official government nor of an institutional character, the associations furnish a natural and necessary means for co-operation among free men, as contrasted to the subservience of commune or hierarchical structure, and thereby permit a more effective dispersal of power than either our vaunted states' rights or the system of checks and balances. A people deeply suspicious of government has, in this intermediate range of organization, developed nonpolitical social tools which should spare the community excessive state control and yet ensure intimate contact between citizen and state.

Here, in the organizational reflection of the manifold functions of the modern, pluralistic community, lies a deeper reality than specific forms of governmental structure. Suppose, then, that we drop this pretense that our political and nonpolitical spheres are sharply separated, and that we insert the associational level into the total picture. Let us, in the following pages, delineate the government of our country as seen from the perspective of an associational commonwealth, for the sake of initial clarity drawing an idealized picture and deliberately emphasizing its features.

This we have in common with all other communities, that once the obscuring shapes of the state itself are stripped away, we live in a world densely populated by associational networks. The number varies from their astonishing proliferation in an industrialized, democratic country down to the few that have so far emerged in a still predominantly tribal society.

Their quality varies from the voluntaryistic ideal of the democracy, through others still partaking of the characteristics of the guild or medieval corporation, to those in the grip of uncompromising autocracy; and yet they all tend to assume rather similar forms because the problems of representing and leading the membership, at this level, remain fundamentally the same everywhere.

Within the freedom of our country the associations not only matured their own characteristic structure and practices to the full, they were enabled to establish a natural type of interaction between their intermediate level and the organs of formal government. Out of the rivalries among major associations emerged a typical pattern of behavior, a *modus vivendi* among themselves, nonviolent methods of resolving antagonistic pretensions through adherence to certain rules of the game. Also out of this interaction emerged a many-sided equilibrium among the groups, one of whose most conspicuous aspects is the balance of power between two major political parties. From the organized groups comes much of the dynamics which power our constitutionally ordained machinery of state, while the equilibrium, by restraining undue pretensions, protects the liberty of all associations and the individual citizen.

Thus far, the picture to be presented will be merely an idealized version of that described by some political scientists. But now let us make a daring assumption, one nevertheless in character with the American conviction of ourselves as pioneers into the future: our governance represents *the* natural political expression wherever the organizational energies of an advanced community are permitted to express themselves freely. Perhaps a certain generalized pattern of political evolution is inherent in the social and economic circumstances of the modern advanced country? Where, for instance, a two-party system has not yet eventuated, we see an incomplete evolution on the road to an associational commonwealth.

Let us test this hypothesis by attempting to trace in considerable detail this supposed evolution of the associational commonwealth in France, Italy, and Germany through the stages of the appearance of the modern type of associations, their increasing representation through political parties, the emergence of an equilibrium, and the establishment of a two-party system. In these countries one may expect to observe such inhibiting or frustrating factors as the tenacious resistance of hitherto dominant modes of political behavior, the presence of segments of the populace not yet ready for the modern association, and strong tendencies toward greater centralization of state authority, due to exigencies of national defense.

These same factors inevitably assume greater importance in many other nations now only in the earlier stages of development. The maturation of an associational system is so indispensable for the proper functioning of democratic government that its success in different countries is roughly proportionate to the degree of associational development. The countries of the world present a panorama of a crude progression of political patterns running the gamut from the most highly evolved to those which have barely begun to respond to the energies emergent in the modern community. For those scarcely on the threshold of the evolution, their politics can be more accurately assessed through an understanding of politics as practised prior to the Western experiments in popular government. (Quite naturally, also, different historical backgrounds will result in widely varying external shapes of the formal government.) Inevitably, a belief in the validity of this generalized pattern of evolution on a world-wide scale connotes a pessimistic attitude toward the possibilities of rapid political progress in some parts of the world, but it also implies optimism over the long-term trend and the temporary nature of inevitable setbacks on the road to free and stable government.

The Communist party is also an association. It bears, from its origins, some of the characteristics of the modern association, and, in the spectrum of these, is on the extreme, as the most centralized, most disciplined, and most power hungry of them all. It stands as the prototype of the association which, reflecting the desperate power struggle of a more elementary political order, has never learned to accommodate itself to the realities of the pluralist community. From this perspective, the contemporary scene can be interpreted as a struggle between the will to power of a single association, intent on remolding the world to its own preferred image, and the society of those associations which are prepared to yield mutual concessions in order to preserve their identities and basic functions. The Communist party failed to achieve power in the most industrialized nations, contrary to Marxist expectations, because the emergence of the associational commonwealth thwarted its egocentric ambitions, and the question still remains open whether Communist dogmatic militancy elsewhere can also be eroded by those assimilative powers that have proven so successful in taming other group pretensions.

Thus far, an attempt has been made to sketch a universal pattern in which we Americans have been enabled to serve as a leader and prototype for the rest of mankind and which would carry with it a greater conviction of its inevitable triumph than does a Marxist philosophy based on nineteenth-century insights into the beginnings of industrial revolution. Presumably the circumstances of the newer technologically advancing communities, creating the same needs and pressures as our own, will gradually stimulate the appearance there also of the contours and dynamics of the associational commonwealth. To the challenge of Communism and its adherents' dogmatic assumptions, we reply, out of our own experience: the history of our times does not center upon the triumphant march of the proletariat; it depicts the migration of all men into a scientific and technological Wonderland; the assumed dichotomy of workers versus bourgeoisie is merely one glimpse of a vastly wider multiplicity of all kinds of groups; the so-called class struggle is a caricature of the realities of associational rivalries; and the Marxist preoccupation with the tyranny of a class-oriented state is only one confused expression for what is actually the inherent appetite for enhanced power of all organizations.

Americans have an inborn fear of excessive political power, and any professed expression of American political thought on the public level must give it a central place in the scheme of things. We tend to be innately suspicious of both associational pretensions and the state itself, hence let us eschew the names of the foes of the moment and seek the villain in a more enduring form, in the very nature of that most necessary instrument of human welfare, social organization itself. The apparatus of an organization is more than merely a passive tool of administration entirely susceptible to precise manipulation by its members or corps of leaders; all social organizations (not only those of the state) tend to take on a life of their own, to follow an institutional rationale which dictates internal centralization and continued outward expansion. Always present in bureaucratic proliferation, this institutional drive is accelerated by periods of crisis and is the most stimulated by conditions of chronic insecurity. Where it finds fulfillment, the aggrandizement of the organization and its directorate assumes complete priority over its original services on behalf of its membership; an organization established as a tool for certain purposes of human welfare then becomes an end in itself.

All groups tend to see their struggles in terms of good and evil, to fight for righteousness against wickedness. Americans are no exception, and if we are prone to see international issues in this fashion, then the same institutional drive which perpetually endangers domestic freedom, can justifiably serve as the specific focus for our wrath against those who obstruct the coming of a world-wide Wonderland. If we have a mission —and it has hitherto usually been the defiance of Old World despotism—it can be visualized as the liberation of mankind from the enslavement of that excessive institutional drive wherein individual freedom is disregarded in order that the populace be used purely as a material resource by an ambitious organization.

A people imbued with a Judaeo-Christian tradition is disposed to clothe its most intense experiences in Biblical phraseology and to battle for the Lord against heathen gods. Though no longer made out of stone or wood, these gods nevertheless persist; whereas men once feared and worshipped the mysterious forces of nature, they now fear what is for them the equally recondite social forces and find an object of worship in the organizational form of the group itself. These modern Baals, carved out of social forces in the form of the state, party, or race by the custodians of the intense institutional drive, provide the leaders a means whereby unity and discipline may be imposed upon their followers. Evil in themselves through their arrogation of divine qualities for functional social tools, the idolaters of pagan gods must also reject the Deity who incarnates the sacred qualities of the human personality, in order to reduce the populace to willing obedience.

Another category of good and evil also now intrudes into our public life, in consequence of the rapid acceleration of the process of change induced by industrial and technological revolution. The ever-present compulsions of our changing circumstances, if ignored, eventually bring their own natural punishment. Living in a complex civilization in which a sense of progress, of an invincible forward momentum, forms a major component, we must accept its resultant moral code— on the technologically advancing frontier of our age, the failure to react in the appropriate direction results in the natural punishment of worsening maladjustments until corrective measures are taken.

Finally, the national state, with its intense institutional drive, has become increasingly obstructive of the energies of the modern economy, has more and more egregiously violated the nature of an emergent Wonderland in its capacity as a sovereign political unit. The United States has always been more than a national state in the Old World sense, capable of absorbing the migrant members of many nationalities and its imperial powers exerted in a manner that preserves self-determination while also relentlessly drawing the nations into a greater union. Americans have felt their land to be a model province of something greater, planetary in scope, that will materialize as we advance into the future. Our associational commonwealth labors, consciously or unconsciously, to apply its developed practices among associations to the international level as well, to reduce the greatest association of them all, the nation, to the quality of an association also, albeit the largest.

Conditions of life and death competition have hitherto spurred the institutional drive of the state. Should the current development of technology now force the state to limit international rivalries to other means than armed conflict, the long-term consequence of international security would surely be a devolution of authority in the national governments of the world. Then, and only then, could the American people hope to see the realization of their deepest craving, a feasible reduction of big government and the lightening of burdens imposed by our present global responsibilities. Perhaps then, too, the American descendant of Old World peasants would at long last be permitted to follow the advice of Voltaire, who made his contribution to the rational spirit of our Founding Fathers, to cultivate our own garden!

In some such fashion can an attempt be made to weave a coherent pattern out of the various ingredients in the political thought and action of the American people. The burden of intellectual endeavor here must be placed on the outline of the whole, rather than on a complete analysis of its parts. Though it is offered entirely in the spirit of one who proposes a hypothesis, any attempt to present a broad explanation for the infinitely complex living reality of the modern political world must necessarily be drawn too sharply, the concepts edged with too much certainty, the selected phenomena engraved more deeply against the background than they are in actuality. The requirements of communication demand a systematic presentation which will inevitably contain the seeds of its own dogmatism; the shears of selectivity will cut too deeply into the living reality of the whole panorama. In order to make certain that the intent not be misunderstood, the narrative is couched in utopian form, a description of the emerging heavenly city on earth by someone who already lives in the modern Wonderland.

A people that leads the world in its command of physical energies and the creation of material goods does not thereby prove the possession of superior governance. When accompanied, however, by an enduring demonstration of successful self-government, Americans must surely have the right to believe themselves also in the forefront of political evolution. We can thus reassure ourselves that our development has kept pace with the times, and that the vision of Tom Paine, at the beginning of our history, still holds true: ". . . to exhibit on the theater of the universe a character hitherto unknown, and to have, as it were, a new creation entrusted to our hands. . . ."

THE INSTITUTIONAL DRIVE

1

THE PEASANT IN
WONDERLAND

The American people seem, during recent decades, to have enshrined the Westward movement of the covered wagon trains as the central theme of our national epic. By means of cinema, and now television, every child participates in the romanticized experiences of the conquest of our continent, while the violent action and heroism, whose meanings are understandable to the least sophisticated elements of the population, quite naturally appeal to the popular mind. One must, nevertheless, suggest the heresy that while the Wild West and the frontier may perhaps be the most colorful and stirring aspect of our history, it is not the paramount drama in the American adventure.

Our country possesses another tradition, one equally filled with the spirit of human adventure, though apparently far less susceptible to portrayal in a popular form — that of The Immigration. This great stream of millions of individuals, which reached its greatest volume early in this century, furnished the hands for the building of a continent and swelled the surging energies of a young people. Reared in the nursery of Britain, the Americans now inherited the racial stock and the culture of all Europe. Quite probably, far more of the authentic America had its origins at Ellis Island, the main gateway to the land of liberty, than in all the wagon trains that ever crossed the prairies.

The overland trek and the ocean voyage had this in common: they were both journeys by men seeking to escape from an unsatisfactory past into a brighter future. Seen from this perspective, the history of the United States is the composite story of the personal odysseys of countless individuals seeking the land of their dreams. Out of the momentum of these two great movements, and the type of human beings created during them, was engendered still another journey — one in which we are now engaged — the migration into a Wonderland made possible by scientific inventions and technological developments. In the creation of a commonwealth on an hitherto unattainable level of material well-being, our citizens are as much pioneers as in the conquest of a continent.

Swedish immigrants in the late nineteenth century sometimes referred to the United States as *framtidens land,* the land of the future, thereby implying that they were moving to a potentially higher plane of existence than that of their former homes. For the peasants out of Europe's villages, the dimensions and awesome energies of the New World excited an astonished admiration, as well as bewilderment at its initial strangeness. Could the inhabitants of the older rural world, in which much of humanity lived for long centuries, actually have seen the emergent modern community — with its control of nature's energies, its economy of abundance, its medical advances, and a governance best expressing its social forces — they would have regarded this novel utopia as a land of wonder, a Wonderland, and the word is used in this sense in these pages.

A development initiated in England and Western Europe in consequence of industrial revolution, the march to this Wonderland has now spread, with dramatic swiftness, into nearly all populated areas of the earth. While sharing with others in the actual process of mastering the energies of nature, Americans have served, particularly, as the advance guard in the building of homes and communities in the modern commonwealth; our experience has differed in significance from that of our confrères in Western Europe because the new forces being released here had greater scope for a natural development in a more malleable society and in a larger, more commensurate, geographical area. We have been an exception on the planet, free to respond to the newly released energies without those inherited burdens which must be borne by most other peoples, and hence enabled to advance the more speedily to the construction of a novel community. We foreshadowed and helped to lead the way for an immigration of the multitudes on other continents into a Wonderland, though it now emerges amidst the familiar surroundings of their own countries.

After many generations of futile utopian dreaming about an ideal community by the more restless spirits, men are now not only permitted, they are compelled to enter a material paradise. Under the duress of a continuing chain reaction of scientific advances, those in the forefront of man's most challenging odyssey must learn the art of living in an emerging Wonderland, whether natively ready or not. This compulsive ascent from one plane of existence to another, with far-flung consequences in every phase of society, is surely the dominating fact of our century.

For those on the earlier stages of the journey, our commonwealth offers a visible, tangible goal, capable of generating a more intense emotional impact than any conceivable rival utopian plan. Not a mirage or dream of a distant future paradise, it exists *now* and reflects most faithfully the fundamental energies of that community toward which all peoples labor. The proven accomplishment makes the pressure to attempt the march irresistible, though some of these others may choose to describe the journey to their utopia in very different terms than ourselves.

When American pioneers brought civilization to a primitive land in the Westward movement, they adjusted to the fundamental realities of their new environment while also transforming their surroundings, and they did so without unduly sacrificing their cultural heritage. The advance into Wonderland poses substantially the same general challenge, though with the important difference that, this immigration continuing indefinitely, each generation must, in turn, face up to frequent feats of adaptation in an ever-altering environment.

This is a matter of brain cells and nerve tissues, a less dramatic but more subtle and exacting process than that of conquering the wilderness. Taken in this sense, the conquest of the West seems like a prologue, cast with more clear-cut figures and incisive action, to the infinitely longer and more difficult conquest of the ways of living in Wonderland. Complex novel problems which must be surmounted replace the mountain ranges across the trails of the pioneers. The wastelands of an illiterate population can pose as deadly a peril for the forward march as did the wilderness of the West. Instead of cutting trees for the wagon trail, the pioneer must

now hack out the rudimentary, oversimplified political reactions which obstruct true progress. Demons in the mind
replace Indians as the enemy waylaying the unwary or unfortunate. Mirages still shimmer their false promises on the
horizon. Each of mankind's journeys, whether temporal or
spiritual, has posed its special dangers, and the peasant setting out on his pilgrim's progress, in this secular age, to a
heavenly city on earth may, instead, wander into an earthly
Inferno.

II

In these chapters the peasant is a symbolic figure for the
human race in the process of migrating from the former
predominantly rural society to the complexities of an urban
community. A large portion of the world's population is now
engaged in making this transition, while even those born in
our most advanced countries must nevertheless acquire the
arts of citizenship in a community too complex for the untutored mind. The authentic peasant is the ancestor of those
who inhabit *our* Wonderland, and he lives on, more than we
realize, in all of us.

One must, indeed, wonder who deserves the greater com-
passion, the man who lived too soon to make the journey
to the golden city of the future or he who is now irresistibly
drawn to face the secular pilgrim's progress of our age. When
the peasant migrates to the new society, or when it comes
to him in his homeland, a mind reflecting the several thousand
years of a normally fixed environment must adapt to novel
circumstances, for the peasant is not prepared in personality
or knowledge to be a citizen of Wonderland.

For many centuries "the peasant masses . . . maintained
an imperturbable sameness . . . unchanging while . . . radi-

cal changes again and again recast the civilization in which they lived." [1] The peasant had been conditioned, over many, many generations, into an habitual pattern of attitudes and values, reactions and responses, which adapted him fully for living in the immediacy of personal relations in a little farming village. The community, embattled forever in a struggle with a rigorous nature, necessarily remained organized in terms of subsistence, each person having his essential place and routine of daily activities as these were dictated by seasonal and village requirements. Inasmuch as change was a dangerous gamble which might endanger their lives, the methods of farming were the safe ones, those proven by past experience. Only by careful adherence to customs which had carried them successfully through the years, only by maintaining a closely knit group, could the villagers expect to survive, for they had a very narrow margin of safety. A belief in conformity, obedience to authority, and respect for the traditional, these principles provided the necessary unifying bonds for that type of society and the natural mental and spiritual accompaniment to the reality in which they moved. Beleaguered by the threats of drought, flood, famine, and pestilence, the dwellers were too deeply immersed in their own moiling in the fields to apprehend substance or sense in the distant, irrelevant existence of politics.

Across Europe and vast areas of Asia, Africa, and Latin America stretched tens of thousands of these kindred communities, an apolitical empire always sundered by hundreds of masters of alien outlook and yet obeying laws of behavior basically similar because these laws were rooted in the nature of peasant circumstances. In the village the inhabitants lived virtually outside of the framework of the state and history. Beyond the peasant's limited horizon, he knew, there moved

---

[1] Oscar Handlin, *The Uprooted: The Epic Story of the Great Migrations that Made the American People* (Boston, 1951), p. 7.

the great ones of the earth. Their presence manifested itself most impressively in the clanking passage of soldiers, in the sound of trumpets, and the beating of war drums. In their wars they came, and plundered, and killed, and upset the endless struggle with nature for sustenance and life itself. From a practical point of view, their actions were senseless to him, if indeed it occurred to him to question events which must have seemed as much God-inspired as nature's storms.

When the peasant moved from the personal security of the village into the modern community, he had difficult adjustments to make. His virtues were not in themselves now sufficient, nor could habitual values be modified as swiftly as the environment. The sons and grandsons of peasants must necessarily retain a portion of their inherited outlook, the mind almost inevitably persisting in its accustomed patterns of thought; though believing that they have rejected their past, they frequently merely put new names to old ideas and assume that change has been achieved.

In place of an orientation based upon one perspective came the confusion of many conflicting viewpoints, while a single set of dogmatic principles was shattered by a weltering incursion of new ideas and values. One truth, based on tradition and time-proven adequacy, ultimately was succeeded by one which encompasses the new multiplicity by being a method, that is, by a tentative acceptance of ideas in open-minded willingness to consider new and contrary evidence, both as a general code of conduct in ordinary life and as a more precise procedure in higher learning.

When he moved to Wonderland, the peasant lost his firmly established niche in society, ceased to be a part of a greater whole, as the village organization dissolved. The large family group, the economic as well as the social unit within the village, also broke up, and the peasant emerged into what was at once a greater freedom and a greater insecurity. Where society had formerly been characterized by a settled uniformity, he now found himself in the midst of a multiplicity of groups and occupations, a bewildering array of organizations, many of which pursued goals at variance with or opposed to his own. The permanent gave way to the transitory, mobility replaced stability, change became the constant order of life, as contrasted to the peasant's instinctive reluctance to adopt any novelty which might prove a costly failure. For one accustomed to the cohesion of a single community, society might well seem to be disintegrating.

The personal regime in the village, the local knight or squire supervising the inhabitants of the little domain, an hereditary family presiding over a village of families, could not survive in the new circumstances. The old relationship, sufficient for the routine of small, static communities, was replaced by government more adapted to managing a changing, pluralistic society, and in time even the ultimate personal symbol, the monarch, often vanished. Having hitherto lived remote from the state, the peasant would now be drawn into it through the revolutionary reversal of political theory whereby authority purportedly emanated from the people, not the lords. Far from simply becoming aware of the looming shapes of this power structure, he would also be required to become an active participant in it, a citizen.

The immigrant entered a more complex society with an infinitely wider range of magnitude, multiplicity, and tempo which frequently passes beyond the range of purely common sense perception or understanding. The forces of the new age, as they had impressed themselves upon the minds of men, had molded institutional forms and practices into adequate, if far from perfect, vehicles for themselves. Parliaments, political parties, cabinet systems, forms of representation, associational influences, law precedences — their evolution had reared an edifice of government not sufficiently comprehensible through elementary observation and common sense. The complex government entailed much knowledge of books, experiences of leadership, a reservoir of political wisdom, and, in the details of administration, a division of labor into specialized techniques practised by experts. Wonderland also required a spirit of adaptation, compromise, tolerance, the mutual adherence to certain rules of the political game. Of all this, the observation of the untrained citizen would tend to be limited to the forms of the institutions and the men who seemed to operate them.

Between the realities of the evolving community of Wonderland and the rudimentary conceptions of the peasant, consequently, lies a great gap. The scientist learned to submit to the realities of nature before he was able to tame it, but men have usually not been able to conform with alacrity to the realities of social energies. These pages deal with the transition to Wonderland, with the gradual adjustments to its pressures, and with the consequences if this does not occur with sufficient rapidity.

When the peasant migrates into a society where its citizens have become habituated to the new order of things, he is absorbed into the established ways. Where, on the contrary, the peasant is confronted with the new society while in the company of equally untutored fellows, his comprehension can only be feebly illuminated by elementary visualizations of true reality. As the immigrant to Wonderland feels the power of organized society impinging upon private life, as the movement of events intrudes upon his own career, an explanation for this pervasive presence in the environment may be sought in a single motive power or irresistible causative factor. Feeling himself at the mercy of the energies of society as he had once been subject to the powers of nature, the peasant might be induced, through the awe and fear evoked by the unleashing of such mysterious forces, to catch glimpses of the demons and ogres, now exorcised from nature, in the surrounding social forces. Gigantic technological energies, in turn making possible social powers on an unprecedented scale, may arouse wonder and dread; as once he worshipped nature's gods, so, for lack of rational understanding of complex social phenomena, the peasant might therein discover and worship new gods. Rational thought may not be enough, is not convincing, and a more colorful and potent imagery, such as apocalyptic visions of a struggle between good and evil, may furnish the requisite explanations for events. Whether the mind of the migrant to Wonderland can immediately mature more than a modicum of political wisdom must be doubted.

Nevertheless, he whose grandfather was a peasant may cherish the aspiration that man will assume an attitude toward the community like the farmer to his cultivated fields. No longer completely a prisoner of his environment, the quondam peasant must learn to judge with an objective eye the good and evil which grows in his new garden, carefully protecting the budding plants which will bear good fruits and eradicating the suffocating weeds of evil. By his study of social and political organisms having learned to what extent their natural behavior can be utilized for his own advantage, he would then tend his fields with eternal vigilance, lest they relapse into a wilderness.

III

Had our continent been a site for man's earlier emergence to civilization, it, too, would undoubtedly have been divided into a score or more of countries, each forever dominated by the tyranny of local geographic factors and perpetually frittering away vital energies on petty warfare with neighboring communities. The farmers of the river valleys, the merchants in the towns, the tribes roaming the plains, the men of the hills, in every region the pressures for the formation of territorial states by the dominant group would have found fulfillment. In Wonderland, however, they are all integrated into a flexible union.

The cowboys of our great Western plains were one form of a social force which elsewhere appeared, time and again, as hordes of mounted invaders pouring into more civilized lands. Soldiers, servants of the state in Wonderland, employed their mastery of physical violence to impose themselves upon the populace as rulers. Mercantile forces that now express themselves in trade along the open thoroughfares once fought their way along the avenues of commerce, and the churches, which repeatedly were compelled to adopt secular practices in order to protect themselves, function in Wonderland as typical associations. Seen from the viewpoint of the old order, America is filled with embryonic forms which under present circumstances can never achieve their full fruition in independence. The perspective in Wonderland is just the opposite, that is, those groups which have a function to fulfill in society need no longer divert their energies to the more formidable problems of survival; hence they may fulfill their intrinsic purposes more appropriately and completely.

We are a people made up of many immigrant peoples, but just as truly, we are a commonwealth wherein almost every conceivable social group that is native to Wonderland lives in freedom to exercise its functions. For Americans, these associations are such a familiar part of the scene that they scarcely require identification or description. We need only pause to reflect about those that each one of us, individually, participate in: a church, an organization representing our occupation, one or more fraternal societies, service groups, and many others, for their names in this country are legion. Whether the name is Presbyterian, United Steelworkers, Rotarian, or American Legion, and however different may be their immediate objectives, their structure, with some exceptions, tends to approximate a common pattern and their official meetings to be conducted in a similar spirit. They vary in size from miniscule local groups of only brief duration to gigantic national organizations, each of whose memberships exceeds that of the total citizenry in many an independent country. They serve all manner of purposes — economic, religious, political, philanthropic, fraternal, scholarly, recreational; their presence in large numbers is the single most reliable criterion that a country has achieved maturity, that it is a legitimate province of Wonderland. The polar extremes among present-day nations are represented in those states which permit adequate expression to an associational age and those which, harking back to older patterns of government, centralize the community under a rigid power monopoly.

The history of the creation of the governance of Wonderland is, in part, the story of the emergence of these associations and of how their characteristic forms and practices were molded by their environment. It is also the story of how they developed an equilibrium of power among themselves that guarantees a relative security and autonomy for all of them, while concurrently offering a larger scope for personal free will in which man to some extent can liberate himself, as an individual, from the massive pressures of his society. A number of generations were required for the original development of this complex society and government, an evolution which in turn was based upon foundations laid in earlier modern times. When the peasant has moved from his old home in areas relatively untouched by this evolution, his migration can truly be visualized as a sudden journey across the centuries from an earlier historical period into the present. Had a sixteenth-century reader of More's *Utopia* actually been enabled to travel to that imaginary land, the immediate personal impact could scarcely have been any greater. This century of the transition to Wonderland when utopian dreams have been realized has, however, also produced strange and awesome deviations from the optimistic expectations of earlier prophets of Progress. Techniques of mass butchery were perfected in two great world wars. Monstrous dictatorships arose out of the heart of civilized countries. Bands of barbarians detached themselves from the normal body of society, and, by seizing the machinery of government, were able to plunder the civilized communities. At times, the continuity of evolution in history, of any rational pattern perceived in past developments and projected upon our present, appeared to be disintegrating, as fragments of a presumably civilized twentieth century floated in the raging whirlpool of events alongside ancient and savage practices. History seemed telescoped when episodes recalling the days of barbarian invaders suddenly incongruously appeared alongside the ultramodern.

Though many reasons could be cited for these unexpected phenomena, some of them are the direct consequence of the advent of Wonderland and the sheer inability to adjust with sufficient rapidity to the imperative pressures of the new order. The authentic peasant is not the only one who must learn to accommodate himself to the ways of a novel community. Now mingling on one kaleidoscopic worldwide stage, in this telescoping of history, are tribesmen of desert and jungle, the surviving aristocracies of an earlier day, mandarins, men with the minds of medieval religious fanatics, eighteenth-century bourgeoisie, nineteenth-century manufacturers, generals of the armed hosts, and the concourse of Wonderland itself. Actors from all the ages have been summoned to speak their final lines in a few brief decades before finding new roles in the commonwealth of a planetary Wonderland.

2

ASSOCIATIONS EMERGENT

Our unquestioning acceptance of the territorial national state as the suzerain lord of our politics has dangerously obscured our vision of those forms of intermediate organization whose continued vitality safeguards freedom in Wonderland. These, too, have had their histories of origins, struggles, and triumphs on behalf of segments of the population. In an age of abundance, when the victories of one group no longer necessarily connote the increasing exploitation of the others, their collective role in the politics of the community continues to be often grossly misunderstood.

Their development in the modern world had been foreshadowed within the medieval cities by the rich growth of associational life. The need for collective action among groups of merchants and craftsmen, particularly, rendered imperative the creation of organizations capable of serving their interests. The multiplicity of their resultant guilds, in fact, forms one of the principal characteristics of the age.

Though originating out of circumstances and needs basically common to all urban communities, these guilds were, nevertheless, in important respects rather dissimilar from the modern association. They tended to be self-contained entities in that each was geared both for the attainment of the highest possible economic welfare of the group in an age of scarcity and for defensive measures against enemies; out of necessity, the associations tended to become states within the state. Their functions were much wider: economic, political, cultural, religious, military. A city guild often exercised such essentially political prerogatives as policing its occupational group, participating in the councils of state, and providing its own contingent for the army. In spirit, the group partook partially of the state and partially of the family or clan.

Compared to the modern association, a much stricter discipline over its members was maintained. Medieval man assumed that everyone belonged to and was bound by a group, that the individual's status and privileges were defined by this membership. Each person became virtually the property of one of these groups, his talents at the command of the association. "In the Middle Ages affiliation with a group absorbed the whole man. It served not only a momentary purpose. . . . It was rather an association of all who had combined for the sake of that purpose while the association absorbed the whole life of each of them." [1]

Small scope for the development of individualism existed

---

[1] Georg Simmel, *The Web of Group-Affiliations,* translated by Reinhard Bendix (Glencoe, Ill., 1955), p. 149.

here, in contrast with the modern, and the movement of the talented toward a higher position in society would be strictly limited. As these organizations grew older, in fact, the chance for advancement in one's own guild also lessened. If the government within such an association as the guild had originally been quite democratic, if the group had come into existence as a brotherhood of equals, such was no longer true after a time. Even as political offices in feudal tenure had become hereditary and as position was stabilized in entrenched oligarchies in city republics, so with the offices in the associations, where leading families increasingly concentrated control in their own hands.

Exigencies of self-preservation molded the association, generation after generation, as it sought maximum protection in a society where law and order often failed, and where obedience of the membership and centralized control in experienced hands seemed the primary requisite for the struggle to obtain security. Obeying the same inherent tendencies of growth as in the political state itself, the association sought incessantly to strengthen its position, to safeguard its prerogatives, to gain a greater voice in the management of the community or the state. This broad evolution ultimately transformed the association into a typical medieval corporation, existing primarily for the preservation of its privileges. Once it had become an unassailable vested interest, the corporation settled into a rigid formal institution impossible to reform and certainly not representative of large numbers of its own disenfranchised membership.

In the earlier stages of its development, however, one senses a groping by the social forces of the later medieval and early modern toward the political solution of Wonderland. The multiplicity of a modern society was, in fact, to such an extent adumbrated by the proliferation of new groups in an expanding economy that Otto von Gierke could call the medieval urban community "a society of societies." The area of the city-state was sufficiently circumscribed to permit the natural groups to exert pressures upon the government, the consequence being the appearance of certain forms and practices that foreshadow those of Wonderland. An astonishing variety of experimentation in popular assemblies, administrative bodies, and distribution of powers occurred in some of these cities. A number of the stronger guilds often set up alliances so powerful that they were able to assume control of the Commune, and other guilds subsequently sought entrance successfully to the ruling circle, in a type of development calling to mind a similar broadening of political representation during the past century. Had the associational rivalries brought into existence a permanent rather than an occasional balance of power — perhaps based upon such traditional loyalties as the Guelfs and Ghibellines in Italy — the resemblance would have been closer. Always following an ideal much more nearly approximating that which now would be called a one-party state, and with the idea of a legal opposition still being impossible to conceive, the townsmen usually transferred political power by violent means, and they were just as likely, later, to reverse the verdict by similar methods. In their inability to maintain the machinery and the habits of modern constitutional government is visible the chasm between that period and ours.

A fumbling for the modern solution is also perceptible in the beginnings of parliamentary representation, which reflect both the attempt and the failure to hurdle the continuing obstacles of a lack of communications and transportation. The more important major occupational groupings found ways to make their voices heard in various European countries through periodic meetings of a States-General, but not yet were conditions ripe for the full fruition of such a development. Within the larger dimensions of the national state, most of the associations were quite unable to create an effective countrywide network of local chapters or to mobilize any cumulative and continuing pressure upon the state. An absolutist government, beyond the reach of social organizations primarily adapted to local circumstances, thus became characteristic of the age.

As the prince steadily augmented his powers, the medieval organizations were smashed, gravitated under such governmental control as to become agencies of the state, or survived primarily as representatives of legalized privilege. A devastating legal weapon for royal aggrandizement was found in Roman Law, which stemmed back to a state recognizing no association aberrant from its own complete jurisdiction; the lawyers now laid this sharp ax to all of the luxuriant associational growth which had not been conceded the right to exist by the suzerain authority. Nor could organized groups ordinarily recruit champions among the reformers, for so strong was the antagonism against medieval survivals and corporate privileges that such critics as the Enlightenment philosophers of the eighteenth century were much more likely to side with the monarch than with the associations.

Unable to break out of an outdated defensive shell, too long habituated to traditional forms to resume an evolutionary development in response to a changing environment, and hemmed in by restrictive laws, the surviving guilds must needs be swept away by the modern state when the pressures of Wonderland began to materialize. National unity was necessary, multiplicity had become tolerable only within its framework, and the modern group would accommodate itself to this spirit with a less exclusive, more voluntaryistic, type of organization.

In areas of the world other than those where Western political institutions had their inception, associations of a medieval cast endured into the first part of the present cen-

tury. In the neighboring Islamic regions of the Levant and
North Africa, for instance, the associations were rather similar
in function to those of medieval Europe. All city dwellers in
an occupation were members of a recognized corporation
which maintained a rigid hierarchy of its members and which
was "self-contained and almost self-governing." [2] Everyone
— artisans, merchants, students, servants, even beggars and
prostitutes — possessed their own guilds. The head of the
organization was usually chosen from an hereditary family
(or possibly the richest man in the group was selected), while
a council of the Masters, or a portion of them, assisted in
the government of the association. No direct role was played
by the guilds in the city government or in influencing it
through their spokesmen, although the municipal officials,
conversely, found the organizations themselves useful as a
means for keeping order or as a tax collecting unit. Further
afield, in India and China, guilds also survived, which to the
Western eye seem medieval in spirit and structure.

II

Although a few of the modern associations derive directly
out of the older type, most of them have come into existence
as a consequence of more recent forces and circumstances.
While some churches have made the transition from the old
to the new, the vast bulk of the modern societies obviously
have no direct continuity with the organizations of late medieval and early modern times. The emergence of the earlier
modern associations is obscure because these were frequently
compelled to seek obscurity themselves from the authorities.
Discerning origins is also rendered difficult by their transitional nature, that is, often originally modelling themselves

2 Hamilton Gibb and Harold Bowen, *Islamic Society and the West*
(London, 1950), Vol. I, p. 277.

after the older type and spirit, they then perforce increasingly assumed the characteristics of the later form.

Conditions seem to have been particularly conducive for the growth of the modern association in Great Britain and her White colonies. In the broadest sense, the protection of the English Channel and the consequent absence of militarism or any stringent compulsion to conformity permitted a relatively free atmosphere in which could occur a more natural evolution of society than was the case in more imperiled communities. On the one hand a greater continuity could be maintained, and on the other the possibilities for the appearance of new organizations, not state directed, would be more auspicious.

Such Englishmen as Frederic William Maitland have proudly written of the long prevalence of an abundant variety of group life in the country.[3] Certainly the spontaneity with which the early colonists set about creating organizations in America seems to argue a deep origin in English life far antedating the formal creation of modern associations. Presumably the organization of joint-stock companies was a reflection of an individualistic spirit of organization which could not be contained or expressed within the prevalent guild form, and which led to the formation of voluntary trading groups in order to achieve by a collective will certain specific business goals. They must, in turn, have served as one subconscious model, a little later, in the creation of the modern associations, with their individualism, their voluntary pooling of energies or wealth for a limited purpose, and their tendency to defy the state when it sought to impose authority.

Definite organizations of the modern type were appearing throughout the eighteenth century. "Combinations" of laborers

---

[3] Frederic William Maitland, "Introduction" to Otto Gierke, *Political Theories of the Middle Age,* translated by F. W. Maitland (Cambridge, 1913), p. xxvii.

were increasingly frequent (they had, in fact, drawn hostile legislation long before this), and the passage of restraining Combination Laws testifies to their growing numbers toward the end of the century. So-called Friendly Societies, created ostensibly for ensuring some degree of social security for workers and their families, appeared in numerous places and, under cover of this, quickly assumed interests in directions more nearly like those of the later labor organizations. Cultural groups were being organized, religious societies within the Established Church were on the scene by the beginning of the century, Chambers of Commerce made their appearance in the latter part of it, and, in general, the incidence of associations rose rapidly as the Industrial Revolution picked up momentum.

In one field, the religious, the obscurity is lifted because religious issues were so inextricably interlaced with the open English political conflicts of the period. According to John Neville Figgis, the Church led the way in the struggle for associational freedom, even though this was obviously not the original intent or proclaimed goal. The multiplicity of creeds was, above all, the immediate factor which thwarted the coming of absolutism in Great Britain. "It was the competing claims of religious bodies, and the inability of any single one to destroy the others, which finally secured liberty." [4] Although the idea of the tolerated nonestablished churches was impossible to conceive even in much of the seventeenth century, the irreducible Dissenters forced, in practice, the admission of tolerance for religious association, though neither as yet complete nor extended to all religious groups. In the long run, the members of the Established Church also were to seek a defense against excessive state controls by claiming the inherent rights of a religious group.

[4] John Neville Figgis, *Churches in the Modern State,* 2nd ed. (London, 1914), p. 101.

Undoubtedly, in molding the form and spirit of the modern association the profound sectarian influence was decisive. The typical characteristics were gestating within the denominations for some time before any legal status was accorded the Dissenters. Whatever their original conceptions may have been, when the sects failed to convert the community as a whole to their own religious beliefs they necessarily espoused the position of voluntary association, that is, driven to the realization that they could not assert their mastery through state power themselves, they claimed inherent rights and liberties for their own group. The sects, by representing the limited religious field in a secularized society, also were reduced to the characteristic restricted goals of the later associations. In spirit, its members were not so much bound by obedience to an association as by a sense of direct, personal comradeship, and the persecutions, which frequently befell them in the earlier stages of development, cemented these ties with one another in the face of the common danger. The supreme expression of this fellowship occurred in their joint participation in the church services, especially in the celebration of the Holy Communion.

Within the group, their government resembled the natural form for small, free groups everywhere, all members participating in the choice of their leaders, while also being strongly influenced by the elders. Equally important for the future, the local congregation quite naturally sought and maintained ties with similar congregations elsewhere, and thus there grew up the typical network of associations on a national level, all held together by common beliefs, purposes, and need of defense against others. In time, also, the sects learned toleration of other organizations and, eventually, a certain degree of co-operation in the community with them for purposes useful to all. The gospel of Christian love and neighborliness was put to direct usage in the community; it was given tangible reality in specific and everyday circumstances in a manner foreshadowing the more secularized activities of the later associations.

These societies blazed the trail in determining the behavior pattern of the future association, the relationship within the group and the approach to other organizations. The omnipresent lodges appeared, imitating the practices of the religious groups, and thereby providing a further source of personal contacts in a mobile society. A secularized personal behavior, derived out of Christian fellowship, provided the binding ties for organizations in which formalistic and traditional compulsions could be safely minimized. Presently the associational movement also manifested itself in the political field with the creation of organized political parties; be it noted that in their initial appearance, in a looser form than actual association, they were regarded as factions shattering a natural unity, just as the religious sects were so originally stigmatized. In this fashion developed the Anglo-Saxon community in Great Britain, in the British colonies overseas, and in the United States with its

> great numbers of private and semi-private voluntary institutions for the common purposes of individual citizens: professional associations, trade unions, charitable bodies, local authorities, and so forth. Such a society is not a series of layers but a tightly woven fabric, each strand an individual citizen or family, but all woven together in a complicated pattern of common life.[5]

As early as the middle of the nineteenth century, Italian writers, searching for the secret of English success that might help to alleviate the plight of their own countrymen, stressed the astonishingly wide activities of the associations as an indication that they were the heart of the solution:

[5] Henry V. Hodson in *The Western Tradition: A Symposium* (Boston, 1951), p. 96.

> Public benevolence, hospitals, asylums, foundling homes,
> savings banks and mutual benefit banks, orphan asylums,
> poor houses, in many regions even the schools, are fruits,
> blessed fruits [of the] spirit of association. . . . And in
> England, which is and always will be in this respect the
> great model country, religious propaganda, the abolition of
> slavery, the abrogation of the grain laws and free trade
> were also magnificent consequences of private association.[6]

Some years earlier Alexis de Tocqueville was being impressed by, and writing about, the role of associations in American life. By the beginning of the twentieth century, the German sociologist, Max Weber, saw in the association one of the chief features on the American scene, and both men believed that American society foreshadowed the type toward which Europeans were also moving.[7] In our own generation, it had been aptly said, "America . . . is simply the framework for as many communities, and as many different kinds of communities, as the people desire to create for themselves." [8]

On the European continent the new type of association seems to have appeared more slowly. The degree of development varied greatly according to governmental policy and the persistent restraints of state church, traditional guilds, and absolute monarchy. Thus, in France, the Huguenots at one time gained a position roughly the equivalent of the English Dissenters because they, too, had proven irreducible, though the absolutist state later became strong enough to crush and disperse the association of Huguenots. Chambers of Com-

---

[6] Quoted in Kent Roberts Greenfield, *Economics and Liberalism in the Risorgimento* (Baltimore, 1934), pp. 310–311.

[7] Jacob P. Mayer, *Max Weber and German Politics: A Study in Political Sociology* (London, 1943), p. 39.

[8] *U.S.A. The Permanent Revolution,* by the editors of *Fortune* magazine in collaboration with Russell W. Davenport (New York, 1951), pp. 55–56.

merce were founded in major French cities, but by direction of Louis XIV and functioning in a quasi-official capacity; contrariwise, we do hear of secret workers' organizations springing up, and the Masonic order, also secret, was growing in numbers and influence.

Wherever the current toward Wonderland began to move swiftly and powerfully, the associations multiplied and assumed functions which in more static communities had been maintained by the state or by the older type of organization. In a society where the people were pushing into new lands or where technological changes were creating new circumstances, governmental supervision obviously could not keep pace; in the very nature of things, the needs and pressures encouraged the appearance and proliferation of associations as an expression of the forces within a dynamically growing Wonderland. These organizations made possible a continuing transformation of the community, new economic interests shouldering themselves into prominence in a constant process of growth and decline of groups within the relatively fluid structure of society. Historical circumstances combined to make possible the rich spawning of free social organizations relatively untrammeled by governmental restrictions.

Nevertheless, such a community could not have flourished without the guardianship of the strong national state and the popular assumptions of common nationality. The political centralization of the modern age assures the security, the law and order, within which the associations can develop in accordance with their intrinsic purposes. Once weapons of violence or extreme coercion are withdrawn from use by private groups, the associations need not be deformed, as were the medieval, by the need for strong organs of protection, a dictatorial leadership, and rigid discipline over the members. Even though in rivalry with other groups, the multitudinous distribution of fields among diverse interests, the very multiplicity of society, forces each association to an extent to cherish the national unity within which they all thrive.

Nor could such a society have emerged without the improvement of communications and transportation brought by industrial and technological revolution. In a medieval city-state, as noted earlier, the major groups could influence the government, for no problem of communications existed. In the national state, on the contrary, most of the associations would be virtually cut off from the capital; marooned by distance, their clamor would be heard only faintly. Improved methods of communication and transportation made possible the formation of networks of associations nationwide in size, and consequently able to bring weight to bear upon the centers of political power. Probably more effectively than the system of parliament itself, this eliminated the basic condition hitherto permitting, perhaps compelling, the forging of the absolute state. Another phase of communications, the coming of universal education, which prepares everyone to communicate and to be communicated with beyond the range of personal contacts, was also a requisite if this promise was to come to full fruition. The social tools were being devised, the human beings activated, for the citizenship required in Wonderland. The nation was growing a sensitive nervous system, which quickly and explicitly transcribed the sensations of the body social in all of its components.

From the major contemporary associations flows a steady stream of publications explaining their individual virtues and goals, and perhaps also denouncing their rivals. The wider view of the entire associational phenomenon, one which embraces them all rather than espousing the limited cause of a single group, has come more slowly. So deeply immersed are the citizens of Wonderland in the whole associational system, so natural and normal does it seem to them, that its broader significance within the political framework, and its contrasts to that which had gone before, usually escapes notice. A development as profoundly important for the democratic processes as constitutions and parliaments became a permanent and living reality before such men as Gierke and Maitland, near the end of the last century, began to place in proper perspective the full sweep of the movement, the political significance of the existence of a multiplicity of associations. Although its practices are visible before us daily, and every realistic officeholder is keenly aware of its constant pressures, not yet has its meaning fully permeated the political thought of the citizens of Wonderland.

As for the great bulk of mankind, it entered the twentieth century as almost complete strangers to the associational forms and practices which are an inescapable concomitant to the technological developments of Wonderland. Then, abruptly, the peasant was thrust into the world of the future, one filled with social forms and energies unfamiliar within his own milieu. Liberated from his closely knit group, the peasant was plunged into a Wonderland of mammoth proportions, where his own horizons had vanished.

3

THE GOVERNMENT OF WONDERLAND

A peasant immigrant, arriving in the American Wonderland, urgently needed to make a place for himself in the new community. He could scarcely resolve his problem through the help of the formal institutions of his new land, in which, for the moment, his freedom often seemed overabundant. The political grouping of citizens into territorial divisions — wards, townships, counties — created few ties beyond those of sheer propinquity and, in fact, emphasized the individual as an unattached atom without direction or gravitation.

Aside from previously arrived relatives or friends, his initial personal contacts were likely to occur within the membership of an association. In the first instance, this might be a church of his own people, while occupational and fraternal affiliations would presently provide him with other friends. The association enabled a man to mingle with people of common background or interests, even though not necessarily living in the same neighborhood. It restored his self-respect and gave him representation, indirectly, among the voices in the public forum of Wonderland.

Unquestionably, the stream of heavy immigration greatly spurred the growth of associational activity in this country. Nor did the termination of the great movement from overseas end this particular type of stimulus, for the restless mobility of the populace within the country, and the constant presence of newcomers in our towns and cities, has, in this respect alone, ensured a continued role for voluntary societies.

Not that Americans need this motivation! Almost any serious issue or proposal of action will rouse, in some citizens, an urge to organize, to institute immediately still another society. Certain types of personalities, apparently, secure endless pleasure and satisfaction, plus fulfillment of their sense of duty, by serving in local groups which perform socially valuable services, though also sometimes deteriorating into the merest busywork. Each of the local clubs furnishes an outlet for the individual where, beyond the routine of his calling, he may exercise his talents and establish a name for himself. Small town or suburban honors are available in the multitudinous offices and committees in sufficient quantity to assure ample scope for self-expression by the average person; for the more ambitious, district, state, and national offices beckon.

Voluntary organization is a natural concomitant for democratic government, it being especially congenial to the temperament of individuals of too much substance, of too much personal autonomy, to serve as compliant pawns of higher authority. Each organization forms a network of human beings obligated to mutual assistance in a community no longer hierarchically directed, where a niche in society is not automatically provided, and where complete individualism poses obvious perils. "Thus, the creation of groups and associations in which any number of people can come together on the basis of their interests in a common purpose, compensates for that isolation of the personality which develops out of breaking away from the narrow confines of earlier circumstances." [1] In arranging facilities for many common interests not provided by the state, men vastly enlarged the possibilities for enriching the life of their community. A citizen of Wonderland, usually a member of several of these associations, joins each group for a definite purpose (or related ones), but his other fields of activity are not thereby directly involved. He does not join as a complete person and is by no means, therefore, entirely attentive to their demands. Within this complex swarm of overlapping, interpenetrating networks, the stronger individual reserves independence of judgment and action.

The elective associational offices, which are usually passed around in order to give each member an opportunity for his day of glory as well as of responsibility, usually carry with them little genuine power. Real control normally resides in the hands of men in the background, who may once have held office, and who are animated by obvious zeal for the goals of the group, enjoy the exercise of power, or simply relish dealing with people. A crudely democratic process governs the selection of this inner circle, a leadership by tacit consent of the others, the result being a natural compromise between human nature and a theoretical democracy where all voices carry equal weight. It is government as old as mankind, rule by the elders.

Usually acutely sensitive to the felt consensus of the whole group, these men provide the authentic continuity within the group, originate the policies, agree upon likely candidates for

[1] Georg Simmel, *The Web of Group-Affiliations*, p. 163.

office, and constitute an informal tribunal which formulates the value judgments for the organization. To them the elected officials must have recourse, if they would achieve constructive results. In meetings of the organization, the business at hand normally moves quickly, for it has been arranged beforehand by informal caucus of leaders; the official sessions are dedicated to the solemn democratic ceremony of passing motions by the sovereign members, of formally ratifying decisions already formulated. Guidance by the elders and the passage of measures earlier agreed upon are even more characteristic of regional and national organizations than of the local groups; and those largest of American associations, the major political parties, are essentially, in their quadrennial conventions, large-scale replicas of what happens in small town clubs at every crossroads in America.

When one of these associations meets — local, state, or national — the government of the people is in session, even though the group is often dealing with minor matters involving only the one organization. The responsible duties of citizenship are here being practised, public opinion is being manufactured, and drives are being generated which turn the wheels of formal government. Frequently the work of occupational self-regulation, benevolences, or civic projects would otherwise have to be carried on by political agencies, or, more likely, would not take place at all. The United States, which has been transformed by scientific and technological developments, is now pervaded, and even increasingly dominated, by these structural channelizations of the various interests and drives of the American people.

II

When former colonial peoples proudly establish their independent governments — when the peasant seeks to migrate *en masse* into Wonderland in his own country — they eagerly grasp for political magic in republican institutions, in parliaments, ministries, elections. Far less likely to be apparent to them is the indispensable function of the association in nourishing and sustaining their democratic practices.

As a contribution to government, the emergence of the modern associational system may, in fact, be as momentous an innovation as, for instance, the original appearance of the cabinet system. Neither development was planned, both drew adverse criticism as a perversion of proper government, but both grew naturally in response to the needs of an age. Whatever its demerits, the association made possible the adequate functioning of constitutional organs of government in a democracy under conditions of industrial and technological revolution. Not only have they, to some extent, helped to prevent an undue agglomeration of power in the state by providing an apparatus for self-regulation and furnishing organizational support for numerous community services, these networks of the most active elements in the country have made representative government much more representative by bridging the gap between populace and authority through setting up effective channels of communication.

An average citizen lacks the wherewithal to exercise personal influence, but the association strengthens the voice of the individual, serves as a megaphone whereby his wishes may be heard in the appropriate quarters. Through agents in state or national capitals, the organized group is able to act on behalf of its members, and any person who speaks for an association, rich in votes, will find that officials listen with attention. In the actual practice of effective national representation for the active functional elements within the country, the spokesmen for the associations come close to being what they have sometimes been called, a third house of Congress.

In the pluralistic society of today, the chosen representative of a heterogeneous population can scarcely satisfy all of the contradictory interests in his own constituency; this defect of territorial representation is to some extent rectified by the ability of national organizations to work with spokesmen from various districts more in sympathy with their point of view.

It has been said that the state is that portion of the population which knows what it wants, and, taken in this sense, the associations represent the genuine power, as contrasted to the unorganized, in this country. It was estimated, in the late 1940's, that over seventeen thousand national, regional, and state conventions, attended by ten million delegates, were being held each year,[2] and in these ten million we see the modern equivalent of the town meeting, the presence personally of people actively concerned with some aspect of the infinitely complex modern society. Today, the classic form of the political state is transfused by the dynamic energies of the associations, which seem to be of virtually decisive importance in determining the direction of policy.

In the very nature of a pluralist society, these groups are in competition with one another, sometimes colliding into direct conflict, though much more frequently in an oblique or indirect manner. Groups representing antagonistic economic interests are, of course, chronically involved in a tug of war. Associations, precisely reflecting the diversity of the community in this respect, are engaged in a constant and many-sided rivalry for membership, resources, favorable public opinion, and influence with the government.

An organization must be able to attract new members, ensure the support of rank and file, and give the individual something worthwhile in return for his loyalty. The voluntary

[2] *U.S.A. The Permanent Revolution,* p. 135.

association presumably lacking the traditional means for compulsion (though by no means always true in practice, especially in some occupational groups), the social pressure to participate and to conform becomes a centripetal force in enhancing the strength of the organization. Each major association must develop its art of persuasion, both for the members and the public, to a high level. It necessarily attempts to universalize its ideas, that is, the members must be convinced that their group and its particular viewpoint on society is vitally needed for the welfare of the community. The more zealous will be unable to understand why outsiders do not accept insights or dogmas, whose cogency from their own experiences in a certain group they feel so strongly; personal orthodoxy is most conspicuous, outbursts of fanaticism by otherwise rational persons most likely, on this level.

Nevertheless, though there is always a hard core of true believers, the members of the modern association do not necessarily march or wheel at the behest of the leaders. Except where their vital interest is most directly threatened, they are unlikely to approach unanimity on any issue. In some instances, in the business world especially, the organization is unlikely to wield as much influence in the community as some of its individual members. The leadership is endowed with the usage of the group name and purports to speak for all, and it is the bearer of the organizational will in exerting as much influence as is feasible, but its capability varies radically from one group to another and on different issues, according to the support that can be mobilized.

The directorate of a national association tends to display characteristics reminiscent of political government. "Trade associations, labor organizations, churches, political parties, all possess a rudimentary internal governmental machinery; and the process of politics and governance within these groups has an intimate kinship with the politics of the state as a whole." [3] Their problems are in many ways similar to those of the state, not only as they seek to reconcile the conflicts of interest within the group and work for a more complete co-operation among members, but as they must devise means for coping with external rivals.

Were any major association permitted to use its power unchallenged to rearrange the community according to its own conception, then the association would become merely an instrument for predatory exploitation of the populace. Or if the rivalry between functional groups, each organization following its own selfish purposes without restraint, were allowed full expression, this would lead to the sort of civil war which the Communists profess to see in the class struggle. Each overly successful special interest, however, is likely to be checked by generating its own organized opposition. On each major issue, the involved interests tend to line up, aggressively or defensively, on one side or the other in a balance of power not altogether dissimilar from that often existing among nations.

The genius of the associational system lies in the cumulative result of the innumerable rivalries, tensions, and alliances among organized groups: the emergence of a many-sided and ever-changing equilibrium of the whole. Out of the operation of this system, out of the process of their learning to live together, has developed the practices characteristic of the advanced twentieth-century community. Here, democracy becomes a tool, a well-proven method of adjusting differences among groups without resort to violence or crushing the individual by the jostling among these groups. A rough equilibrium exists, with the tensions and pressures being somewhat mitigated by acknowledgment of certain rules of the game.

Superimposed upon the national equilibrium, in turn, are

[3] Vladimir O. Key, Jr., *Politics, Parties, and Pressure Groups,* 2nd ed. (New York, 1948), p. 79.

the political parties, which channelize the diverse energies and direction of the different organized groups. The parties have evolved into vehicles for implementing the wishes of the associations while simultaneously checking and limiting the excessive demands of the individual organization. The party, the "great common denominator of American society and economy," unites "the largest possible number of divergent interest groups in the pursuit of power," it "integrates a vast number of conflicting interests in an organic way" by forcing compromises and conciliation below the governmental level.[4] Where the process of evolution has been completed, the political equilibrium is climaxed by the achievement of a crude balance of power between the two major coalitions; in countries where the various interests remain unreconciled, however, the incomplete fusion of the nation is likely to be reflected in the presence of non-democratic parties in a multi-party system.

This equilibrium is constantly changing, in long-term trends, as certain groups grow or decline, antagonisms sharpen or moderate, or the leadership of any given association alters in aggressive intent. The democratic network of political and associational representation is the equivalent of a nervous system for the nation, whose various groups, despite their rivalries, are as dependent upon one another as the parts of the human body. The appearance of distress in any portion of the equilibrium will presently affect the entire structure when the groups directly involved react with increasing restiveness to their troubles. Countries often apply placebos or political drugs to alleviate the problem (incompetent governments do so much too often), but are constrained to more

[4] The three quoted passages are, successively, from Henry Steele Commager in *Living Ideas in America,* edited by H. S. Commager (New York, 1951), p. 194; John Fischer, "Unwritten Rules of American Politics," *Harper's Magazine,* Nov., 1948, p. 32; and *U.S.A. The Permanent Revolution,* pp. 122–123.

effective measures if it continues. A democratic government is perpetually preoccupied with the necessity of preventing areas of discontent from intensifying or spreading, lest the entire national body be jeopardized.

When an accumulation of discontent is nevertheless permitted to pile up, the balance of power may shift perceptibly and thereby initiate a period of relatively drastic political action. Injustices and maladjustments are, of course, always present in any society, but a pronounced worsening of economic conditions or the rapid growth of new powerful interests, the cumulative effects of growing incongruity, will cause a major era of reform, in the actual sense of re-forming the society in accordance with the contemporary pressures. Thus a properly ordered democratic society seems to oscillate politically between periods when the emphasis is on adjusting to new forces and conditions, which in Great Britain and the United States seem to come approximately once in a generation, and intervening periods dominated by impulses toward consolidation.

Changes which do occur are normally relatively mild, even in years of reform. The groups which suffer a loss at these times are not sufficiently damaged to resort to violent means of retaliation. They always have the hope that the restraining pressures of the equilibrium will presently modify their losses and the next election will permit them to recoup their positions. One may contrast this with the revolutionary situation where alterations have not been effectuated gradually and at the proper time, and where a long series of frustrations prepare the way for disaster. Once reforms of a fundamental nature occur here, they in turn will trigger other changes in a cycle growing more desperately violent as the very existence of some groups is threatened.

Realistically appraised, one must conclude that the perpetual and ever-changing balance of power among associations wittingly or unwittingly safeguards liberty against the state and the presumptions of any group. Though it is perfectly patent that aggressive behavior often yields undue privileges, eventually the balance of power hardens against further encroachments. Our constitutional separation of powers and the residual authority by the states are intended to preserve liberty against any threatened power monopoly, but they have long since been supplemented by the wide diffusion of community energies and responsibilities among the nonpolitical organizations. Within the spacious dimensions of a continent, the forces of Wonderland found social organization in the association — and within the surprisingly capacious framework of the American constitution the latter grew vital functions, quasi-political in nature, which have greatly assisted in the fulfillment of an authentic democratic government.

III

Numerous criticisms of the associational system, in part or in its entirety, could be cited. Many of those in a position to comprehend its nature fail to do so because they are absorbed in the affairs of their own association and therefore do not see the total picture. Most citizens quite naturally resent the obviously self-centered activities of the major organizations and their lobbies — except their own. Reformers impatiently continue to look directly to the instrumentality of the state and its agencies as the quickest way to achieve their goals; these would, with the thinkers of the eighteenth century, claim that associational privileges are in themselves a major bar to continued progress. Some would assert that any conception of an equilibrium is old-fashioned, that the preponderance of state power already makes such a theory untenable. Like Harold Laski, who once believed in the important role of the associations, still others have held that their influences are minor by comparison with the overriding economic dictates of capitalism in action.[5]

Despite their deep involvement in the associational system, Americans tend to focus their attention directly on the relationship of the individual to the state, and they do so primarily because the assumptions of a general nature will continue to remain so firmly rooted in American political thought. V. O. Key points out that the concept of an equilibrium or balance of power among groups of different interests is foreign to American ideology, for we believe that government by the people should be government by the people as a whole, without any organized intermediaries.[6] We permit our high regard for our traditional political principles to obscure a proper appreciation for the tenacious quality and enormous value of the associational rules of the game which have developed within the larger framework. We minimize the American contribution of the past century and a half, the product of a free society at work and the spontaneous creation of our political genius under the tutelage of forces at work all over the world.

The alternative to the associational system, under present conditions, is the bureaucratic state, teeming with regulations, whose frequent effect in specific application is that of tyranny. The ultimate consequences of this alternative were described in the latter half of the last century by Hippolyte Adolphe Taine, whose criticism of the Bonapartist or first modern dictatorship still remains highly relevant for our own age. Arguing against the usurpation by the state of functions better lodged in the associations, he asserted that when the state itself is in trouble it halts or reduces the services it has undertaken to render, that state officials will use the services

---

[5] Herbert A. Deane, *The Political Ideas of Harold J. Laski* (New York, 1955), pp. 153–154.
[6] V. O. Key, Jr., *Politics, Parties, and Pressure Groups,* p. 6.

for self-aggrandizement or incompetent persons will be appointed, and that the state must necessarily operate through uniform laws and detailed regulations whose applications are too rigid or mechanical.[7] To this must now be added the only temporary efficacy of even salutary measures, which presently becoming outmoded thenceforth increasingly hamper the further evolution of the situation regulated, and yet, in their institutional quality, are apt to be even more difficult to modify than the vested interests of any given group.

For substantially the same reason, the continuing domination of a community by one association, such as a single political party, or a group of interlocking associations, will increasingly violate the nature of the modern society. In the words of Alexis de Tocqueville, written over a century ago:

> Those classes continue to form, as it were, so many distinct communities in the same nation; and experience has shown that it is no less dangerous to place the fate of these classes exclusively in the hands of any one of them, than it is to make one people the arbiter of the destiny of another.[8]

Whatever the circumstances bringing them to power, and even though they represent the direction of development, they will nevertheless affront or stifle the growing individuality of other groups, including those nourished by their own activities. Modern society has become too complex for any group, or any one man, no matter how benevolent, to hold power over any extended period of time. Only the interplay of many points of view, the representation in the state of all the active elements, can bring a rough conformity with the pressures of the age.

Not that the associational community offers perfection!

[7] Hippolyte Adolphe Taine, *The Modern Regime,* translated by John Durand (New York, 1890), Vol. I, pp. 117–119.
[8] Alexis de Tocqueville, *American Institutions,* edited by Francis Bowen, translated by Henry Reeve (Boston, 1870), p. 305.

The natural order of a pluralistic democratic state which emerges in Wonderland may, in the final analysis, possess as many faults, proportionately, as its predecessors in their proper places in history, and it obviously breeds its own varieties of injustice. The justification for the associational democratic community, nevertheless, the unanswerable *raison d'etre,* is that it alone combines the preservation of individual freedom with a capacity for adjusting to changing circumstances. Evils that flow from its rejection or stultification increase in magnitude as Wonderland, in other respects, grows in power.

> Pluralistic empiricism knows that everything is in an environment, a surrounding world of other things, and that if you leave it to work there it will inevitably meet with friction and opposition from its neighbors. Its rivals and enemies will destroy it unless it can buy them off by compromising some part of its original pretensions.[9]

In these words of William James we find the philosophic expression for the hard reality against which one-sided political crusaders, who would universalize their creeds, must campaign vainly. The open or covert struggle between groups, so much a part of human history, has been metamorphosed by the development of the democratic associational system from a series of conflicts by violence, rebellion and repression, or actual warfare, into a species of pressure and tension which restrains the emergence of any group that becomes too strong, prevents any group from taking on the attributes of a state within the state, and protects the individual member in that organization.

In an age of incessant change due to technological advances, society must assume a form and provide a process which allows alterations with a minimum of major conflict and violence. The response to this need is the utilization of

[9] William James, *A Pluralistic Universe* (New York, 1909), pp. 90–91.

"temporary" organizational units, the associations, which in their individual growth and decline serve as vehicles for the varying and ever-changing social forces. In a community whose economy and technology are constantly evolving, a rigid framework is impossible, for not only is society now much more complex, more fecund of many diverse groups, the configuration of power itself alters relatively rapidly. Hence the association serves as a base which contains and makes possible modifications without disrupting society; it assures the necessary cohesion and continuity while permitting flexibility. Earlier practices, institutions, symbols lose their vigor when certain organizations cease to support them or are themselves no longer in a position to enforce their wishes. Meantime, new associations have appeared, virtually unnoticed by the public, which may serve as bearers of innovations, new practices, the seeds of the future.

The advocacy of the associational system by no means implies support for the special privileges of a few powerful organizations; on the contrary, these privileges are much more likely to arise from the failure of a part of the community to employ the associational tools and methods. A group skillful in using available devices for enhancing its own position has a great advantage only so long as those injured by it do not themselves resort to the available and obvious countermeasures in order to restrain excessive pretensions. The existence of special interest groups is a fact of life of the modern community; they cannot be abolished without substituting the omnipotent state, and the only feasible alternative is the full implementation of the associational system in order that all voices in Wonderland be effectively heard.

Within the present context of Wonderland any basic conception of a Right and Left tends to become an optical illusion. As someone has said, the Right need not necessarily be the sole custodian of the shrines of the nation, nor does the Left necessarily march as the vanguard of the pilgrimage into the future. Political terms coined in an earlier milieu — liberalism, conservatism, and others — no longer adequately or precisely express the meanings to be conveyed, for we have moved into a new frame of reference, into a new political environment, where the old terms and broad generalizations have less and less validity. The large Estates have disintegrated, and we have neither masters nor oppressed. Minorities, as such, are losing their meaning because, in a sense, every group has now become a minority. To be sure, each group tends to line up on one side or the other of the associational equilibrium according to its own perceived advantage in the acceleration or the retarding of change, but this distinction is far from clear-cut in practice.

The real political dividing line, in the modern nation, is that which separates the adherents of the normal community and those who, for one reason or another, would step outside of it. Those fanatics who refuse to perceive the actual contours of the contemporary community or to recognize the compulsions of an evolving Wonderland, in seeking to frustrate its natural energies would inevitably compound evil by their actions.

The validity of the criticism mentioned earlier can be better judged in the perspective of associational evolution, both in its stages of emergence and in those current tendencies which portend lines of possible future development. The Anglo-Saxon countries, a number of European states, and a few others have undergone successfully the several generations apparently necessary for the maturation of associational democracy. Many other countries are now painfully groping their way in the same direction, whatever their momentary political terminology may be, because similar pressures drive them, despite temporary deviations, in the same direction that we have gone. An examination of the pattern of evolution as it unfolded in France, Italy, and Germany should provide more detailed insight into the nature of the associational system, as would a following survey of other countries where the potential for a successful completion of the pattern in the near future is less promising.

Other aspects can best be evaluated in the light of current tendencies. The principal virtues of the system undoubtedly have lain in its spontaneous origin and in its not yet having been formally introduced into the actual structure of the political government. The growth of gigantic associations, their tendency to centralization, and the existence of exceptions to the voluntary principle raise the question whether the modern association has merely been going through the early stages in an evolution kindred to that of the medieval guild and that the future will see them assume characteristics increasingly reminiscent of the late medieval and early modern corporation. This, in turn, opens up the question of a phenomenon which is herein referred to as the Institutional Drive, and which forms the principal theme in subsequent chapters.

4

PATTERNS OF POLITICAL EVOLUTION

Only through a lengthy process of evolution can a complex government so deeply rooted in its community as that of Wonderland fulfill its potentialities. Certain developments must take place, each largely dependent upon the success of the preceding one: the older type of association must be replaced by, or be transformed into, the modern form; these need to find a means of expression through political parties; and the mutual accommodation of the groups should be reflected in a political balance of power. While the Anglo-Saxon communities have achieved the archetype of such government, their experience in its creation is not entirely relevant for other countries because only in rare instances is the modern associational pattern elsewhere enabled to emerge to fruition through a relatively facile evolution.

Much more typical were the developments in such countries as France, Italy, and Germany where the same dynamic forces have produced substantially the same results under more difficult circumstances. Here, also, the forces bred by industrial and technological revolution imperiously asserted themselves, breaking through the crust of rigid forms and insistently working the malleable stuffs of society into forms more consistent with their own nature. In these, however, traditional groups and long entrenched modes of political behavior offered formidable resistance. Underlying progress toward the new society was oftentimes obscured by violent political upheavals — wars, revolutions, dictatorships — and the new forms frequently continue to bear the distinguishing markings of their ancestral communities and the scars from their birth throes. Their experiences are characteristic of those faced by the majority of nations as they strive for a modern governance. If certain features in the evolution of each of the three are successively scanned, problems and stages of development will be recognized which constitute the present for other countries and which, one may surmise, also tend to foreshadow their future.

Turning, then, first to France, we find a striking contrast to the Anglo-Saxon nations in the long-term effect of the traditional groupings, both in their actual survival and (perhaps even more) in the tenacious memories of their opponents. The older corporations were obdurately antagonistic to some aspects of the new order, and this animosity, in turn, generated such enduring hostility to the existence of any intermediate bodies between state and citizen that the evolution of the new pattern was hindered. This situation was to be repeated in many other countries where the coming of the new age brought massive assaults on traditional vested interests, and where these, by reason of an obtuse insistence on maintaining the ancient privileges of a vanishing age or an understandable reluctance to lay aside old defenses and entrust themselves to flimsy guarantees of an unfriendly state, fought back with all the means at their disposal. Not only were the old corporations swept away, but as a consequence, their resistance also laid their legitimate body of beliefs open to attack.

For a number of reasons, of which state domination was probably the most important, the vitality of the associations in France had been so vitiated as to leave them little more than fossil organizations. To such a point had they atrophied that the Enlightenment reformers ignored Montesquieu's proposal that they be revitalized. On the contrary, because they seemed to be purely representative of special privileges rather than the appropriate voices for segments of society, all of the reforming emphasis was in favor of the abolition of existent associations; the *cahiers,* just prior to the Revolution, made no claims for the right of forming associations.[1] In direct reaction to the persisting division of society into groups and corporations long outmoded, arose the concepts of the unified nation and of the general will.

During the French Revolution the egalitarians sought to remove by fiat the intermediate bodies between the individual and the state, and, although they themselves established clubs and societies, when new associations, such as artisans' groups appeared, these, too, were forbidden. Support for these actions came, and would continue to come in the future, from those who erroneously could only see the association in its traditional form, leading directly to privilege, inequality, and

[1] Beatrice Fry Hyslop, *French Nationalism in 1789 According to the General Cahiers* (New York, 1934), p. 93, footnote 173.

disunity. The repeated demands by the representatives of the corporations for such a status accentuated the determination of the egalitarians.

Even during this initial assault, however, the roots of some of those associations which were so abruptly cut down in the revolution were still very much alive and sending forth new growths, that is, the need for occupational organizations of some kind remained constant despite triumphant ideologies. Lawyers, doctors, butchers, and bakers received permission from Napoleon to re-establish guilds, and the masons, shoemakers, builders, and some others also petitioned, unsuccessfully, for the same right during the Restoration.[2] In addition, new organizations, products of the Industrial Revolution, would soon begin to demand recognition. The revolution in 1848 brought a prolific growth of associations, the city workers in this period regarding them virtually as a panacea for all evils; in the guise of mutual aid societies, they were at first encouraged by the republican government.[3] A change in attitude soon followed, however, as the societies very quickly tended to go beyond the expressed purpose and become centers of resistance to employers and to the state. Nor were the workers in all instances competent to run their fellowships.

Regardless of governmental attitudes and restrictions, the tendency toward associational groupings grew in direct proportion to the appearance of elements creative in Wonderland, improved systems of communication and transportation, urbanization, and the extension of literacy. Legal or not, more social organizations were founded. The economic and technological changes themselves were relatively gradual.

[2] Matthew H. Elbow, *French Corporative Theory, 1789–1948* (New York, 1953), pp. 17–19.
[3] Henri E. Sée, *Histoire économique de la France: Les temps modernes, 1789–1914* (Paris, 1951), pp. 238–239, p. 341.

Compared to the United States, the difficulties lay, as previously indicated, in the presence of tenacious patterns surviving from the older era; the new forces would encounter greater obstacles and follow a more devious pathway in order to emerge into their natural forms. Even as the impact of the French Revolution caused an erratic series of alternating extremist movements in politics, so the original rash violation of normal evolution among the associations threw the subsequent developments off center. On the one side the loyalty to older forms would be strengthened, on the other the fear of *any* associational groupings was intensified, and the basic conflict lay between these extremes.

Those organizations which were in more direct lineal descent from the *ancien régime,* the Church especially, continued to some degree to maintain the older attitudes of the relationship of the individual to the group: the more tightly disciplined organization for the sake of defense, involuntary and permanent membership of the individual in the association, the claim of organizational monopoly within the field, and insistence on their beliefs as universal dogma, which in turn limits the possibilities for compromise with others. In their attitude toward the state, they usually favored a certain amount of decentralization, a community more in accordance with what they presumed France to have been before the advent of the absolutist Bourbon state. Catholic political philosophy, particularly, expressed the viewpoint that the "various natural groups of which human society consists — families, towns, trades or professions, churches, etc. — all possess by natural law, a private area of activity in which the state must not intervene." [4] Not only was this viewpoint fundamentally less statist than that of the majority of the presumably democratic following, these spokesmen

[4] François Goguel, *France under the Fourth Republic* (Ithaca, 1952), p. 160.

were also less statist than the advocates of the so-called corporative theory in other countries. Partly an inheritance from the medieval theory of autonomous corporations, this position had also been elaborated as a reaction to their travail with the centralized republican state, and, having experienced the unpleasant aspects of arbitrary, unlimited state power, they expressed themselves accordingly.

That the anti-republican Right should so strongly argue the case for associations may be ironical. Perhaps it was also historically appropriate that it should, for the medieval concept of the place of associations within the community must surely have lain in the background of thought in European countries, such as England, where the modern organized group appeared in certain fields with comparatively less resistance. That is, the traditional elements represented by the French Right might well, theoretically, have provided a more suitable foundation for the evolution of an associational system, had not its own outmoded form, the corporation, and the implacable hostility aroused by it precluded such a development.

Emerging forces of democracy tended to equate liberty with freedom from the obligatory ties of social organizations. Some of the most ardent supporters of the republic were the strongest advocates of the general will in the nation, and this overly statist viewpoint long prevented the allocation of a proper place to the association in their theories. The very fact that Rightists were producing ingenious schemes based upon them, but with an accompanying political philosophy that was anathema to the democrats, would tend to discredit the idea itself among these people.

In actual practice the bourgeois associations, in the form of loose societies, developed with relative impunity under the tacit toleration of the government. A law in 1884 whereby persons of the same profession could form a society for economic purposes consequently only confirmed or legalized an already existent situation. Another law in 1901 completed the freedom of association for political, social, cultural, and economic activities, the sole exception being made in the realm of religion. The only requirement, otherwise, was the filing of a statement of aims and a copy of the bylaws with the central government. During the Third Republic all kinds of organized bodies appeared, ranging from powerful economic groups like the Comité des Forges, representing the metallurgical manufacturers, and the laborers' confederation, the C.G.T., through societies for such groups as journalists, artists, engineers, physicians, teachers, and army officers. The French established, in the words of Carlton Hayes, a "multiplicity of private associations and societies for almost every conceivable human activity. . . ." [5]

By the time that the Radical Left mounted its great anticlerical assault upon the Church at the beginning of the present century, the issue no longer involved the existence of associations, but rather the *kind* permissible in a modern democracy. In effect, the government sought to destroy any surviving vestiges of the Church as a corporation, to relegate it to the position of other organized groups. By the provision that Church property was to be held by "associations for public worship" the very basis of ecclesiastical organization of the Church, the keystone of the whole edifice, would be seriously weakened. The last remnants of a pretense to monopoly were challenged with the withdrawal of state support or any other advantages over religious sects, while claims to the right of supervision of the whole man were rejected in the ending of clerical control over marriages and the school system, the latter already weakened by earlier legislation. Special groups hitherto forming part of the armament of

[5] Carlton J. H. Hayes, *France: A Nation of Patriots* (New York, 1930), p. 196.

the Church, such as the monastic, found themselves severely curtailed. Here, then, was the climactic episode in the emergence of the French associational system.

Not that this in itself, essentially a political campaign, would be responsible for the victory of the new type. Forms and habits harking back to the earlier naturally persisted, in a country of many traditional practices, at a level not subject to the full impact of revolutionary political changes. All of the groups involved in the transformation into a modern industrial France have quite probably been influenced to some extent by the earlier institutional patterns.[6] The relatively slow economic changes and the failure of any subsequent violent social revolution contributed to comparative gradualism in social habits. In the case of many of the organizations, patterns created before the democratic processes had been fully accepted yielded by degrees to a changing reality. Only the incessant pressures and practical exigencies of the twentieth-century community would transform associations, which originally usually looked back to the ideal of the guild, into the more or less typical modern form. The Church, also, while regaining some of its lost ground, in practice at least accommodated itself increasingly to the organizational mode of behavior of the republic.

One sector of society, the working classes springing out of the Industrial Revolution, posed a problem in assimilation and have continued to do so. For a long time the French worker was inspired by the syndicalists, whose concept of social organization could be considered an adaptation of the traditional older form to the industrial scene. With the memories of '48 and '71 and under the protracted hostility

[6] John E. Sawyer in *Modern France: Problems of the Third and Fourth Republics,* edited by Edward Mead Earle (Princeton, 1951), p. 310.

of a bourgeois government, the Socialists would obviously tend to retain their ideas of class struggle and a unitary state. In the more recent period the Communists have perpetuated this outlook, and the existence of a large bloc of Communist voters has made the achievement of a democratic associational system more difficult.

During the course of the Third Republic the associations more and more assumed roles very similar to those in the United States. Although the process of assimilation of associations within the system remained incomplete, the next stage in development was far advanced as the groups found expression on the governmental level through political parties. Hayes commented, during the twenties, that the parties' "primary purpose is to champion the special interests, professional, economic, or political, of particular groups of Frenchmen. . . ." [7] Writing about the period between the two world wars, Shepard Clough asserted that the associations "have been reflected with almost mirrorlike accuracy by French political parties." [8] Thus the Republican Federation and Republican Democratic parties espoused the policies of the businessmen, the Socialist program was much like that of the C.G.T. (Confédération Générale du Travail), the Radical Socialists represented the lower middle class, and the list could be extended further. Most of the groups were federated into national organizations, complete with officials, publications, and annual conventions. They were now able to influence the government of France in much the same manner as in the United States, their lobbies exercising constant pressure and their spokesmen alert for legislation which could help or hinder their organizations. If anything, the

[7] Carlton Hayes, *France: A Nation of Patriots,* p. 206.
[8] Shepard Bancroft Clough, *France, A History of National Economics, 1789–1939* (New York, 1939), p. 296.

French parliament of the Third and Fourth Republics was too responsive to the organizations, without the compensatory pressures of a two-party system to modify their pretensions. The size and influence of interest groups had reached such proportions in the Fourth Republic that, at times, they almost seemed to overshadow the political parties themselves.[9]

France was unable during either of the two regimes to take this final step, the establishment of a two-party system in which one exercises power while the other stands in loyal opposition. Whereas American and British groups compromise their differences on the party level, the French continued to do so at the top, in the cabinet itself. The involvement of too many political groups, which in a two-party balance of power would assume at least temporary roles within one of the major parties, compelled the constant usage of coalition government. Such a ministry is too dependent upon a wide sweep of political organizations — Center and Right or Center and Left — for any enduring common policy to be adopted. In these circumstances, decisive action becomes almost impossible, and paralysis of government threatens to follow because it is too easy for any one group to veto a measure by the mere threat of withdrawal from the alliance.

Undoubtedly one factor contributing to this situation was the simple fact that paralysis of action suited the mood and interests of many Frenchmen. After the Second World War, for instance, business groups which did not want change were allied with those rural elements which were suspicious of governmental power. In a more general sense, the existence within the population of a considerable segment which does not look to politics for salvation makes effective political organization difficult and reduces the opportunity for co-operation among groups, the more so since the individual

[9] Gordon Wright, *France in Modern Times: 1760 to the Present* (Chicago, 1960), p. 537.

organization tends to think primarily in terms of its own particular defense against state action. Where this view is maintained, democracy is apt to retain its oldest revolutionary meaning, namely that it consists primarily in "the resistance of the citizen to power and, therefore, of resistance to government." [10]

Inasmuch as the multi-party system is prevalent in a number of countries, particularly in Europe, other factors, not so historically French as the foregoing reason, must also be involved. Thus, France, like a number of others, still suffers from past antagonisms which, going beyond normal rivalries and rendering groups mutually exclusive, make common action difficult. In the prevailing mélange of groups where the differences are still sharp, the ability of the individual to belong to numerous associations is reduced; the network of individual loyalties, which binds all society together, performs this function less adequately. Group interests have become too rooted; each has built up its own traditions too fully to be able to compromise its interests more completely on behalf of the mutual welfare. One may suspect that the failure to evolve beyond the stage where the major groups are represented by different parties can be explained, at least in part, by a deep-lying persistence of the more intense instinct for self-preservation of the self-contained corporation. Even though they have given up the bulk of their traditional protective devices in structure and practice, the associations remain reluctant to abandon this final tool of defense against other groups or state power and entrust themselves to the protective equilibrium of all national forces.

Another reason for the survival of the multi-party system lies in the personal stake in the maintenance of a particular party by the inner circle of politicians. These leaders, being the most devoted to party tradition, doctrines, and discipline,

[10] François Goguel, *France under the Fourth Republic,* p. 152.

are much more prone to reject compromises than are the voters or parliamentary deputies. Decisions made by the party heads are therefore likely to accentuate differences among the groups, rather than reconcile them, as occurs in the two-party arrangement. The political vested interest is here on the side of the multiple system, unlike in the United States.

Finally, the total failure to assimilate some groups hampers the taking of the final step in the creation of a political balance of power. That is, the continued survival of groups who persist in the revolutionary tradition of intransigent rejection of the present community, and who find in nondemocratic politics identification with their environmental mood, makes difficult the creation of a loyal opposition. Not only will their presence almost inevitably force the others into an alliance against them, this threat of abnormal practices will tend to inhibit the proper functioning of the entire system. The unrelenting working class alienation from democratic practices removes from the normal equilibrium a very large element which elsewhere, as in Great Britain, Germany, and Japan, often constitutes the bulk of one of the two parties.

In the Fourth Republic all parties except those of the extremes were compelled by the menace of the Communists to find common ground for co-operation. One possible line of evolution would have been for blocs of parties of this kind, which form an ephemeral and inadequate substitute for a national party, to merge into a permanent union wherein the participating groups are finally reconciled on the party level. Only a short step separated the blocs from the confederacy of groups to be found in the Christian Democratic parties of Germany and Italy after the Second World War. Equally possibly, the emergence of a nationalist party (such as occurred with the founding of the Fifth Republic), if it were successful and continued to work within the republican framework, would induce the creation of a second major party; the middle groups, caught between Right and Left, might be compelled to submerge their differences and enter into a permanent combination.

As it was, in 1958 France stood ominously near the denouement which usually occurs in less advanced countries with a multi-party system, the exasperated imposition of a *strong* government which would sweep away the numerous parties. Because the major groups would not take the final step in evolution, they were imperiling entirely their right to autonomy within an associational democratic community. A period of grave national emergency highlights the greatest weakness of a plethora of parties, the inability to reach agreement on swift, decisive action, and France, under the pressures of the Algerian crisis, came dangerously close to adopting the course which a community in peril oftentimes finds necessary, the establishment of an authoritarian form of government, such as Italy and Germany had possessed in the preceding generation.

Though the Republican Charles de Gaulle did not establish a dictatorship, his policies, as well as the atmosphere of the Fifth Republic, were hostile to the survival of a multi-party system. Thus, contrasting the national interests of their own following with the particularist emphasis of their opponents, the president and Michel Debré, the first premier, repeatedly inveighed against the "feudalism" of the traditional parties. If their exile in the political wilderness proved to be a lengthy one, these groups might eventually be persuaded to submerge their differences in favor of a unified party capable of once again winning power. The survival of a strong presidency, dependent upon the support of a genuine national party, would manifestly also strongly militate in the direction of a two-party balance of power.

II

Italy's pattern of evolution is roughly parallel to the French, though with certain important differences which have a bearing on the development of many countries today. Because Italy was a newly created nation with a less advanced economy, its problems have greater relevance for those peoples whose circumstances are rather similar at present. Its experiences, promising political progress followed by setbacks, underline the difficulties encountered during the inception of the associational system.

A variety of societies antedated unification in Italy, including groups like the Carbonari, Mazzini's *Young Italy,* and the Masonic lodges, which were forced to operate secretly because of their political aims. Some bourgeois associations of an economic nature also appeared, such as the society for the Encouragement of the Arts and Crafts established in Milan in 1841. In the same period as in France, mutual benefit societies made their appearance among the workers, their usual functions being the maintenance of funds for the sick and aged as well as seeking work for the unemployed. In 1863 there were 453 workers' fellowships, ten years later over a thousand, and in 1885 about four thousand of them.[11] Agricultural syndicates appeared in 1864.

Many of the mutual benefit societies had been instituted by followers of Mazzini, and as early as 1861 he was proposing a nationwide organization of workers. Quite naturally, however, the political disunity in the peninsula would be reflected in the local or regional size of the original groups. Even after the establishment of the Kingdom of Italy, their provincial nature tended to be sustained by the survival of

---

[11] Carlo Sforza, *Contemporary Italy: Its Intellectual and Moral Origins,* translated by Drake and Denise de Kay (New York, 1944), p. 149.

regional differences and interests; indeed, many associations might feel a sharpened sense of self-identity under the pressures emanating from beyond the old boundaries. Nevertheless, the growth of a network of communications and transportation would increasingly make possible the creation of viable *national* associations.

Following in the footsteps of more advanced nations, the Italian community eventually proliferated all kinds of societies, as various groups found organization useful or imperative. Some were national in scope, some were not, but they were in a condition of relatively free rivalry. Gaetano Salvemini, in effect, portrayed an adequate associational foundation in numbers and variety when he began his book, *Under the Axe of Fascism,* in this fashion:

> During the half century of free government in Italy, associations of every sort sprang into being: clubs for political, religious, philanthropic, sporting, educational, and recreational purposes; societies for mutual aid; co-operative societies of consumers and producers, co-operative buying associations; building societies; trade unions; associations of industrialists, landowners, bankers, professional men, civil servants, priests, teachers, and students; associations of ex-service men, disabled soldiers, etc.[12]

Patently, in view of the subsequent fascist fiasco, a spectacular growth of associations did not guarantee political success. They must needs be absorbed into the national life, find a proper equilibrium among themselves, and discover fitting outlets for political expression in the parties of the time. The latter, in turn, should become national in size, giving sufficient, but not excessive voice, to each group. Only through years and decades of experience could the democratic rules of the game take on a reality reflecting the true circumstances of its society.

[12] Gaetano Salvemini, *Under the Axe of Fascism* (New York, 1936), p. 2.

Like so many other European countries in the nineteenth century, and like so many quondam colonies in the twentieth, the original political framework of Italy was modelled on the English. The product of a lengthy evolution was here adopted before it could be fully adapted. Copying forms of government, or installing a liberal-conservative party system, did not guarantee miracles. Political practices will inevitably seek the level of the nation itself, and this occurred in 1876 when the Right, comparatively skillful in administering good government, gave way to the so-called Left, to men of the people. Though the transfer of power seemed to spell retrogression, Italian politics, as Benedetto Croce puts it, now descended from the realm of phraseology to reality, whereby the Italian government functioned more in accordance with the actual circumstances within the country at that time.[13] It was a necessary, if unpalatable, transition toward a more positive, workable form of political life. It also parallels the usual disillusioning, though temporary, occurrence in countries at this stage of development when the original founders of the state lose control to more fundamental internal forces.

Italy in this following period provides an excellent example of the typical early stage in the development of parliamentary government, one in which a number of the colonial countries liberated after the Second World War quickly found themselves. Regardless of the theoretical excellence of constitution or high calibre of leading statesmen, the ingredients for a modern democracy are not yet fully present, and in such cases politics becomes *personal,* revolves about strong men and their followings. This had also been true of England in the eighteenth century, and in France in the period, especially, from 1815 to 1848. Interestingly enough, a government of personalities is often assumed to be the ideal type by the

[13] Benedetto Croce, *A History of Italy, 1871–1915,* translated by Cecilia M. Ady (Oxford, 1929), p. 9–12.

founding generation, that is, statesmen are expected to legislate and act in balanced, moral wisdom on behalf of the
nation, rather than serving as representatives for groups. Even
in the most advanced countries, it tends to remain the rather
naive prototype in the popular mind against which are contrasted prevalent practices. As it seems to work out, however,
government during the personal stage turns into something
very much less beneficial.

In Italy political parties speedily disintegrated into cliques,
each following one outstanding leader. To a considerable
degree, this development was simply an extension of customary practice, in the South more particularly, whereby
clients had grouped themselves around patrons in a relationship which was informal and yet effective. The members of
parliament became primarily agents intent on procuring
favors for their followers or sponsors; patronage held the
gangs together. Far from being the voice of either nation or
segments thereof, the lobby normally sought benefits for
individuals, while the vested interest of the deputies lay in
the privileges of the group as a whole, in their access to the
riches of governmental power. No tangible opposition could
develop, as stronger men were repeatedly placated by being
brought within the charmed circle of governing ministries.
In this stage of development, a democratic regime, unsavory
and corrupt, can come perilously close to being a racket and
may arouse the disillusionment and disgust of sincere citizens,
who may be tempted to turn to some other form of government for a salutary remedy.

"Parliamentary currents were scarcely affected by national
opinion . . . but were mere eddies and gusts within the
Chamber of Deputies and its lobby." [14] The national legislature
could hardly rise above this level until organized channels

[14] Henry Russell Spencer, *Government and Politics of Italy* (New York,
1932), p. 27.

were created through which opinion might be communicated to the elected representatives. Existent parties tended to be identified with localities or, even more, to designate merely the political gang of a particular leader. Not only was additional political experience necessary, effective parties were unlikely to emerge until well-organized associations provided substantial impetus from the active elements in the nation.

As for the associations themselves, they increasingly required an effective system for expressing their needs, reconciling their rivalries, and channelizing them into a workable unity. In time, Italian political life began to move into the next stage of development in democratic government where the self-interest of associations induces their establishment of political parties to represent them or else causes a tie to be sought with one of those already existing. The result would be a multi-party system much like that in France. No less than twelve parties held parliamentary seats in 1922, and their multiplicity undoubtedly contributed greatly to the paralysis which made Mussolini's seizure of power possible. Although they still partook, to some extent, of the nature of personal followings, they had also assumed a greater identification with specific groups, the Liberal Democrats thus representing the old conservative Right, the Agrarians speaking for the landowners, and the Radicals (vanished by 1922) trying to serve as spokesmen for the lower middle class.

A potential national party, more thoroughly organized, appeared on the scene in the eighteen-eighties with the Socialists. The community reacted violently, however, to the intrusion of a group whose aims and practices clashed with the basic nature of its society. In so doing, it behaved in very much the same manner as other national bodies, not yet fully democratic, when first confronted with a group not fitting into the established order of things. The original organization, the Independent Workers Party (founded in 1882), was ordered dissolved by the government in 1886, and when Socialists gained control of the workmen's union in Sicily but were unable to restrain their excesses, the government repressed them brutally. A year after the founding of the Italian Socialist party in 1893, Crispi ordered all socialist associations dissolved, the leaders to be thrown into jail, and their newspapers closed. These organizations were quickly reconstituted when Crispi fell, only to be once again dissolved by government order. Eventually, in 1899, the government tried to introduce legislation which "gave power to the magistrates to dissolve associations deemed to be provocative of disturbance. . . ." [15]

The next phase in the struggle is illustrative of another characteristic of the evolution of the system: public opinion was alienated by the attacks upon the Socialists, the genuine liberals believing that the assault upon one group constituted a precedent-making violation of the basic rights of all, and a coalition of groups therefore rallied to their support. In the victory of this bloc, for the government lost the ensuing election, the general security of *all* associations was enhanced. A few years later when the Socialists called a general strike and seemed to abuse their privileges, the process asserted itself against them, and this time a coalition was formed *against* the Socialists — an associational balance of power, in an amorphous fashion, had momentarily materialized.

Equally hopeful, though it also proved illusory, was the first manifestation of their absorption into the national community in the sense that at least some of them responded to the active sympathy of other groups by moving toward an acceptance of the rules of a democracy. The leaders were more likely, however, to accept the democratic procedures than was the rank and file because economic circumstances in

[15] Benedetto Croce, *A History of Italy, 1871–1915,* p. 209.

Italy prevented the wholesale conversion of Socialists to democracy that occurred in many countries; class hatred and the violent overthrow of their "oppressors" continued to correspond precisely to the feeling of many living under severe hardships. Later this would manifest itself in the support for Communism in the working classes and the continued ambivalence of the Socialists both before and after Mussolini.

While one possible source for a major party remained refractory to assimilation, the other likeliest source was also temporarily blocked by the papal policy against political organization of Catholics. For decades continuing the protest against the loss of temporal authority during the unification, the papacy insisted that it was "not expedient" for Catholics to participate in politics. Although this by no means was successful in preventing Catholics from so participating — in fact the Church eventually to all intents and purposes rescinded the ban — it did hinder the formation of effective organizations.

Catholics themselves disagreed widely, of course, on political issues. They also differed in their attitude toward associations. As in France, some favored the ideal of the guild and tended to visualize the formation of corporations somewhat along the lines of those in the later Corporate State, wherein employer and employee were both represented. Pope Leo XIII's encyclical *Rerum Novarum* expressly permitted labor the right of social organization. Catholics encouraged the formation of co-operatives and finally, in 1918, merged the Catholic trade unions, in competition with the Socialists, into a labor confederation which soon possessed a membership of considerably over one million.

Under the leadership of Don Sturzo, a true believer in democracy, some of the politically active Catholics after the First World War founded the Popolari. This party, whose establishment marks the organized origin of the Christian Democratic movement subsequently imitated in other countries, was built upon the national federations of co-operatives and trade unions of Catholic inspiration. Not intended to be a mouthpiece for Catholic interests like the Center party of Germany, its purpose was to serve as the vehicle for the expression and activation of the social and political ideals of Catholicism. In the 1919 elections it won a hundred of the 508 seats in parliament.

In the Charter of the Popolari occurs a key passage which expresses remarkably well the spirit and ingredients of the associational system:

> For a centralizing State, seeking to restrict all civic and individual activity, we would substitute, based on constitutional guarantees, a State truly popular in quality, recognizing the limits of its activity, giving consideration to the natural centers and organizations of the country — the family, the classes, the Communes. . . . [The party demands] the liberty of class organization without government privileges or preference for any particular party. . . .

> This ideal does not seek to disorganize the State but is essentially organic in the renewal of energies and activities which should find their coordination, valuation, defense and progressive development at the center, shaping themselves into vital nuclei able to check or modify forces of disintegration . . . and draw from the heart of the people the elements of conservation and of progress, giving its value to authority as at once the force and exponent of the sovereignty of the people and of social collaboration.[16]

At this point the prospects, theoretically, seemed favorable that the Italian parliamentary and associational system was about to take another step forward. Out of the multi-party system could well have come a balance of power in which

[16] Carlo Sforza, *Contemporary Italy: Its Intellectual and Moral Origins,* pp. 250–251.

the Socialists and Popolari were the most likely to serve as centers of gravitation. Calculated to further this end was the deliberate policy of Giolitti, who, in Carlo Sforza's words, "believed that all factions, all interests would end by finding an equilibrium in the heart of Parliament." [17] Further enhancing the prospects, a government of moderate Leftists seemed quite feasible as a result of the elections of 1921. Although the government intent was in accord with democratic, associational behavior, the catastrophe of the great war had aroused an internal convulsion, forces had been unleashed, that soon would topple the still fragile structure.

Had the intrinsic strength of the Italian associational system now been greater, elements of disruption might have been contained and absorbed. Giolitti's policy of permitting the forces of the time to work themselves out could only be successful if a balance of power at last produced decisive action, and whereas a coalition of moderate groups, plus some responsible statesmanship, would have prevented the success of the extremism of Right or Left, these parties were as split among rival groups as ever. The Popolari, after a promising start and while actually holding the balance of power in 1920–1922, failed to exercise the expected influence, due to the inexperience of its members and the fact that the party was not yet sufficiently welded together for decisive action. Without them, defensive unity was unattainable among the members of the potential bloc. Furthermore, a papal decree at the beginning of October, 1922 ordering the priests to refrain from political activity, while good in intent, was disastrous in consequences because it weakened the Popolari and the whole parliamentary government at a crucial moment.

Equally unfortunate, the Socialists were evidently not yet prepared to assume the requisite position within the democratic community. A description of the Socialist deputies

[17] *Ibid.,* p. 166.

as "disciplined soldiers fighting on a national scale" who "were individual ciphers in a large, effective total sum" [18] indicated a type of association still far removed from a democratic form or spirit. The workers had recourse to practices, a long series of strikes and generally irresponsible conduct, which in scope and duration were hostile to the welfare of the community and had thrown the weight of public opinion against them. One powerful association in a nation which does not follow democratic rules may force (or panic) other groups to undemocratic tactics also. While the majority of the Italian population might be content to await the erosion of the workers' will by their failures, the most affected elements, exasperated, were quite willing to tolerate or support an equally undemocratic reaction on the part of the Fascists. Nor did the secession from the party of the gradualist or moderate elements, those willing to co-operate politically with the bourgeois parties, have any marked effect upon the course of events.

With two of the essential factors in the situation unable or unwilling to participate fully in an affirmative direction, a semi-paralysis of government ensued. Lacking a persuasive or compelling structure of tangible forces within which statesmen could formulate decisions, the government was now necessarily guided by the equation of personalities in key positions. Perhaps the king should not be censured too harshly for now turning to the man who seemed to him to be the one positive element in the situation. At this stage of development the failure of leadership and the self-interest of parties may still disillusion many honorable patriots; the ship of state seems rudderless, and the temptation to follow a strong leader may become irresistible. In a sense, the Fascist Duce appeared to be, at the time, a throwback to the more personal type of politics, the leader with his followers who are held together

[18] Henry R. Spencer, *Government and Politics of Italy*, p. 47.

by a desire for spoils of office rather than by specific issues and ideas. This was the unexpected sequel to the long development, that under the pressures generated by the war the maturing system suddenly collapsed, and out of the more elemental reactions came a retrogression to more primitive political action.

That the Fascists were something more than a reversion to an earlier political phenomenon, or that they were simply ardent nationalists (as many thought), speedily became apparent. Over a period of years, not only parliamentary government but also the network of associations were swept away. To the absolutist mind of the Fascists, the autonomous organizations seemed an indication of weakness and division in the nation, and, furthermore, they could serve as centers of resistance to the Fascist regime. According to Herman Finer, Mussolini's ideas of the Corporate State developed partly out of the need for destroying the natural groupings, especially the "associations of workers which afford their members the daily opportunity of information, discussion, and resistance." [19] Hence the Fascists systematically smashed all opposition centers, workers' especially, but then used the same tactics on the others until the whole network was obliterated.

Even after the storm had passed and Italy returned to more normal government, the associational political system was still not complete. The Christian Democrats were eminently suited to combine many elements within their single national party, though, very possibly, the continued lack of a loyal opposition has caused them to stretch over too many groups. Socialist traditions and the poor economic level of parts of the working classes continued, for years, to block the full entrance of their groups into the democratic community and to prevent the formation of a functioning two-party system, despite efforts by responsible statesmen in that direction. Only

[19] Herman Finer, *Mussolini's Italy* (New York, 1935), p. 493.

in the early 1960's did Pietro Nenni's Socialists accept a more constructive role than a position of opposition in alliance with the Communists. In Italy, as in France, until the workers were admitted economically into Wonderland, they refused to enter it politically.

Italian experiences emphasize that the path of political progress does not lead straight to the promised land. Relapses will occur, and unfortunate as these may seem at the time, the Italian events also indicate that a Mussolini does not spell the final end of development. Only in the perspective of many decades will the line of evolution ordinarily come into focus before the eyes of the historian, and from this standpoint the palpable faltering in the political evolution of any contemporary nation need not be grounds for undue discouragement.

III

One other question posed by the Italian experience looms even more markedly in the case of Germany, and that is whether a democratic associational system can, in the long run, possibly survive the consequences of modern war, both in its impact upon the groups within the nation and in the governmental centralization it inevitably entails. Industrial and technological revolution swept over Germany quickly in the latter part of the nineteenth century, producing a community powerful far beyond its narrow base in the middle of a continent. Small wonder, then, that this was the nation which should epitomize the tensions of the age, and reflect the forces, penned up in national compartments, as they sought release by violent outward explosion.

By reason of their location forever fearing stalking enemies, real or fancied, beyond the frontiers, the Germans were also, of all continental peoples, probably the most prolific in number and variety of associations. One writer called Weimar

Germany "the land of organizations." [20] Descriptions of associations and their practices by Georg Simmel, based chiefly upon his native environment, read very nearly as though they were drawn from American examples, and equally striking, to the American reader, is his designation of "the web of group-affiliations" as forming the prevailing texture of his society. Perhaps, also, Max Weber was impressed by the prevalence of American societies because they were so familiar at home. Once its massive industrial development was under way, Germany must be deemed as potential of an associational community as the United States — with the profound difference of being acutely subject to a set of geographical factors only operative in America in the most recent years.

Within this amazingly variegated community of many interests, the typical German thoroughness achieved a notably intense degree of group organization in co-operation of membership and in functional efficiency. This, in turn, speedily brought the characteristic pairing of certain major groups with responsive political parties. The original Liberals and Conservatives, like parties elsewhere, had their inception as exponents of certain political ideals, but subsequently "became social groups which no longer struggled for some abstract general principle, but for class interests." [21] In keeping with the degree of associational organization, this becomes clearly apparent earlier than was the case in Italy and France. So true was this that the politics of the German Empire reflected less its status as a federation of territorial states (as had been expected) than its growing character as a federation of competing parties bespeaking economic, social, and religious interests.

[20] Godfrey Scheele, *The Weimar Republic: Overture to the Third Reich* (London, 1946), p. 32.
[21] Henri Lichtenberger, *Germany and Its Evolution in Modern Times,* translated by A. M. Ludovici (New York, 1913), p. 168.

Thus, the Conservative party became the representative of those older groups, the landed gentry, the peasants, and the artisans, who feared the rise of the capitalist influence. Behind the party stood the very powerful *Bund der Landwirte,* the organized spokesman of the landed interests, and also a very considerable portion of the Protestant clergy. The Liberal party, based originally upon doctrines typical of nineteenth-century liberalism everywhere, underwent a transformation between 1850 and 1870 which caused such groups as the artisans to leave it, in fear of the new industrial powers, while the strongest element now became known as the National Liberals and was supported by business interests; those who still upheld to the greatest extent the original principles continued to maintain a separate party organization. As for the National Liberals, the societies established by mercantile and manufacturing groups, like the *Zentralverband Deutscher Industrielle,* found in them a faithful voice. The Social Democrats, with avowedly ambitious political goals, were soon linked with workers' trade unions and their mass following. Finally, the Center party served as the voice of the Catholic Church and its interests in a country with a Protestant majority.

Up to this point the associational system was a promising one, albeit perhaps *too* well organized for a properly democratic society. Worthy of note is the fact that the parties of united Germany, unlike the Italian, never constituted the following of one man; their political evolution did not pass through, on this level at least, the personal stage. The Germans had achieved functioning political parties and gained experience in using them. The type of government which Bismarck imposed upon the Empire, however, the absence of a parliamentary ministerial system, gave less opportunity for normal interplay among the parties, and hence this area had *not* developed in company with the rest of the evolution.

Responsible for the constitutional arrangement primarily, though not exclusively, were the mandatory compulsions of the international situation as the founders of the Empire saw them. Pressures from without, circumstances of intense rivalry and necessities of defense, had the customary effect upon a social unit, that is, such conditions encourage the centralization of authority and the inculcation of obedience among its members. Almost inevitably, the persistent tension of an alert stance in anticipation of attack will curtail liberty of conduct within the community and increasingly bring all groups under state control.

Already in the original acts of Bismarck these imperatives are quite evident as he flouted the will of the Liberals for ministerial responsibility to Prussia's elected representatives in order to strengthen the military. Whatever ideological or traditional justification might be presented, the fundamental necessity, for Bismarck, was freedom of action by the authorities to manouevre as they thought best on the chessboard of Europe. The circumstances of the sovereign state dictated the necessity of continuity in planning as well as speedy decisive action in international affairs. By subsequently building into the imperial structure provision for a guiding power virtually unhampered by parliament, he thought to ensure Germany's position among its neighbors.

Where the administration and this making of policy were fully in the hands of executive and bureaucracy, the members of parliament were unlikely to mature a sense of constructive responsibility beyond their own group. Practices of forming coalitions or reaching compromises were not mastered, nor had the cogency of the new dispensation impressed those elements which had been adequately protected within the Imperial regime. As a consequence of the type of government during the past half century, the abrupt disappearance of the traditional keystone of state in 1918 found the parties ill-prepared to assume the tasks of a parliamentary democracy.

Before the Weimar Republic had been overthrown by the Nazis, George N. Shuster could go so far as to say that "the new Reich was an infant which survived because the arms which supported it were knotty with the sinews of a thousand *Verbände* [associations]." [22] He also depicted a normal associational democracy when he described the societies as "often directly affect[ing] the process of government," in that they were consulted in the drafting of legislation, in the influences they had upon the political parties, and in the active part played by group leaders in political life.[23] On the other hand, the failure to devise an effective mechanism for legislation or for determining policy at the top level is evident in the presence of sixteen different political parties in the Reichstag at the end of 1930 and in the participation of twenty-seven (!) of them in elections that year. Once again it is clear, as in Italy and France, that in this stage of development the national community is subject to the peril of an excessive assumption of political individuality by groups preferring not to entrust themselves to a more inclusive national party machine.

Here, also, the vigorous growth of organized social bodies, coinciding with the coming of democracy, stimulated an assertiveness as yet untamed by a community equilibrium. With many of the smaller, it was a matter of insistence in maintaining a direct political voice within a republican regime, while others, cherishing their own prepossessions of total state control, flatly refused to conform to the democratic rules at all. From its initial years, the Empire had not been conducive to the acquisition of more conciliatory attitudes or the art of compromise. "Bismarck never understood the function

[22] George N. Shuster, *The Germans: An Inquiry and an Estimate* (New York, 1932), p. 11.
[23] *Ibid.*, p. 71.

of politics in modern society and never approved the sense of give-and-take, of compromise, or mutual respect, of representation of the many conflicting legitimate interests for which the function of a political body is to allow adequate scope." [24]

His long conflicts with the Roman Catholic Church and the Social Democrats are conspicuous examples of this. In seeking authentic unification, he drew the lines of nationhood too narrowly, refused representation to those outside of those lines, and used methods which, in turn, could only harden the determination of the groups attacked. With the coming of the Republic, however, it was the Center and Social Democratic parties, along with the Democrats, which formed the core of republican strength. These were the ones who had learned that organized groups "can live together in peace only by learning the ways of compromise, of respecting the view of others, of accepting defeat without recourse to violence." [25]

Because of the bitter struggle with Bismarck's regime, the Center continued to be wary of an all-powerful state; it had been an experience calculated to renew an appreciation of its inherited Catholic concept of the value and rights of associations against the central authority. Furthermore, during the second half of the nineteenth century, Catholicism had nurtured a number of societies within its own fold, which brought greater intimacy with its people.[26] More than any other, this party included persons from all sectors of society.

Having undergone an even more severe harrying by the state, the Social Democrats could also, despite original Marxist doctrines, comprehend the virtues of freedom of

[24] Eugene N. Anderson in *The Struggle for Democracy in Germany*, edited by Gabriel A. Almond (Chapel Hill, 1949), p. 14.
[25] *Ibid.*, p. 24.
[26] Henri Lichtenberger, *Germany and Its Evolution in Modern Times*, p. 234.

association. Some of their leaders helped initiate the movement in the ranks of international socialism toward Revision-
ism, that is, responded to liberalization of the bourgeois society by reforming their views along more evolutionist lines.
At one time feeling the sympathy of the liberals when attacked, the party also suffered the sting of defeat (in the
elections of 1907) at the hands of an electorate antagonized
by their methods. Despite the strong discipline of the membership — the structure of the Social Democratic party was
originally modelled on that of the Prussian army — they were
now comparatively ready for a republic. The Social Democrats, as well as the Center, "knew how to reconcile and
settle conflicts within their midst by reasonable means and
a respect for divergent views." [27]

Had Germany been given a generation in which to practice
parliamentary methods, one could have anticipated a gradual
adaptation or reconciliation of at least some other groups to
the new system. Successful survival would have constrained
a widened acceptance of the reality and values of democratic
rules, though a two-party system (such as increasingly
emerged in the Bonn Republic) could scarcely have materialized without the stimulus of a major crisis or shock. Even
though the German evolution was still far short of completing
this phase of development, another step, not yet attempted
in the most advanced countries, was undertaken with an
experiment in integrating associational interests into the
state machinery. In 1920 an advisory Federal Economic
Council was set up with 326 members, most of whom were
selected by functional associations. Agricultural interests
and industry were each represented by sixty-eight members,
commerce, banking, and insurance had a total of forty-four,
handicrafts, consumers, and transportation were assigned

[27] Eugene N. Anderson in *The Struggle for Democracy in Germany,*
    p. 16.

between twenty and forty seats apiece, while smaller groups had correspondingly less seats in the Council.[28] They voted by groups as well as by individuals, and an outvoted minority could appeal to the government. An institution of this kind could possibly in time have evolved into a type of third House of their parliament, one where the haphazard economic representation that occurs in the territorial would be replaced by direct and weighted apportionment for major groups. Conceivably foreshadowing the ultimate forms to be taken by the forces struggling to emerge within the territorial parliamentary system, it constituted the type of tentative experiment which, multiplied manyfold in various places, will, through the selective process of success or failure, ultimately initiate another stage of evolution in political life.

Although Germany had adopted, in the Weimar Republic, a regimen theoretically in harmony with the features and forces of Wonderland, such a government presupposes the minimum conditions of Wonderland, both in domestic and foreign aspects. The Germans were not given the needed generation of time, and those unassimilated to democracy found their ranks swollen by victims of inflation, depression, and injured nationalist feelings. In a country where the state had previously played such a preponderant role, the impulse of both extreme Left and Right was to solve the problems by seizing the instrument wherein power was concentrated and using it in a dictatorial fashion for their own advantage. Direct action, furthermore, appealed to those not yet habituated to democratic methods, such as that lower middle class out of which were to come so many of the men and attitudes of Nazism.

Elements in Germany continued to vocalize the nationalist imperative for a strongly centralized state during a republican

[28] George P. Gooch, *Germany* (New York, 1925), p. 300.

regime less adapted to international rivalry than its predecessor, and they assumed their most virulent form with the Nazis. Conditioned by the four years of warfare in the First World War, the latter transplanted the psychology and methods of the battlefield to the domestic scene, where techniques utterly foreign to the civilized community were employed against groups who, trained in a very different kind of political rivalry, could not fight back by similar methods. Vastly reinforced in numbers by depression-fostered recruits, and emboldened by the lack of cohesion among the democratic parties, the Nazis came to power — helped by a lucky throw of the dice of historical chance. With them, as with the Italian Fascists, the exigencies of the competitive international order took total priority over the needs of the normal community.

In the broadest sense, the Wilsonian peace had held axiomatic the existence of the national state while also seeking to restrain its arbitrary exercise of complete sovereignty. In practice, the required international order failed to materialize sufficiently rapidly, and Germany suffered the ruinous results of war and the continuing economic hobbles imposed by the artificial moats of political frontiers. The requisite conditions for Wonderland were not fulfilled, the sovereign national state reigned supreme, and the Germans responded by reverting to the logical conclusions, pushed to their extreme possibilities. If a nation shall be united, it must be completely united with all men working for common goals rather than pursuing divergent and conflicting interests. If a country's economy shall be limited by cramped boundaries, and boundaries must exist, then let those boundaries be expanded by force until ample *Lebensraum* is achieved. Nazi conduct reflected the ultimate implications of the existent international behavior, its values and practices exaggerated to the point of travesty at the expense of the normal community. Hitler's Reich provided a hideous alternative to Wonderland, the consequences of ignoring the imperatives of the modern society on the international level.

IV

From the foregoing survey of European countries, it becomes apparent that the two problems before which the evolution falters in advanced countries are the establishment of a two-party balance of power and the final assimilation to democratic practices of all major groups. The former is less serious; indeed, this step need not be taken at all where the number of parties is limited and where, as in some of the smaller European nations, the ability to maintain a mutual accommodation approaches that evinced by groups within a national party. The political equilibrium then manifests itself in the balancing of a governing coalition by a loyal opposition. For that matter, no evolution should continue to the point where two organizations possess a monopoly at the polls. As is clearly apparent in American and English history, a third party serves useful functions: a challenge to the complacency of the major parties, a means for registering the individual or group protest vote, a vehicle for the enunciation of principles or programs not yet deemed politically advisable by the larger one.

Much more of a problem are those groups which remain recalcitrant to the suasions of the community equilibrium. Almost always, the danger is compounded by the weaknesses of a multi-party system wherein it is difficult to take a resolute stand against the threat. Fundamentally, this situation is characteristic of nations at a stage where politically vocal elements are themselves at different stages of development, all reluctant to give up political identity, but otherwise ranging from those eager to participate in parliamentary coalitions to those who remain altogether outside of democratic practices. In less mature countries, the combination is apt to make democratic government inoperable. Nevertheless, where conditions permit, the assimilative processes do work to moderate and convert organizations to the advantages of full co-operation within the system.

Working class organizations, for instance, in their Marxist form emerging through a violent revolutionary movement, fought a parental society whose imminent dissolution they anticipated. Thinking to meet violence with violence, and conceiving of the class struggle in terms of warfare transposed from the battlefield to the city streets, a leader like Bebel could organize the German Social Democratic party on the model of the army. Within a community arbitrarily sundered into two warring camps, the Marxists introduced the tactics and strategy of manouevering social groups in order to seize the citadels of power and thereby initiating a sequence of events leading to the apocalypse of world revolution. Lenin and his Russian Communists pursued this concept to its ultimate degree.

Nevertheless, the workers' groups of western and northern Europe, yielding to a community whose social fabric became stronger rather than weaker, mellowed where genuine democracy made this feasible. If their security within the existing order was assured by legal freedom of association, and if the road remained open to piecemeal fulfillment of their program through the ballot, their antagonism gave way to co-operation. In this way the workers' groups accommodated themselves to the forces and pressures of Wonderland, but only where they were permitted to share in its material progress.

Roman Catholicism had been geared by its many centuries of existence in a more crude society to the attainment of security through the traditional corporation. Accustomed to the proximity of a state normally in friendly hands, the Church necessarily shied away from the prospect of a regime whose leaders were often declared foes of its power, and who proposed to sheer off the surviving attributes of the corporation. Anti-clericalism and the rival ideology of nationalism would drive the organization even more in upon its own resources, seeking more centralized control as well as greater obedience from its members.

Catholic groups first adapted themselves to the new practices in areas where the traditional outlook was less prevalent. The Irish Catholics, grasping the English-wrought device of privately organized societies for public purposes, used O'Connell's Catholic Association to bring about emancipation, and this organization "showed itself magnificently adapted to become a political machine within the procedures of parliamentarianism." [29] After Belgium had become independent, a Catholic political party immediately established itself as an association within the parliamentary framework. During the 1830's and 1840's such liberal Catholics as Charles Montalembert in France and Ignaz Döllinger in Germany attempted to convince other Catholics that the Church could function very successfully under a parliamentary regime.[30] They held that freedom of press and education would give Catholicism decided advantages. Belgium was often cited as an example, while the success of American Catholicism also tended to influence the European attitude.

Basically, Catholicism had carried out of the Middle Ages, as already noted, a belief in the existence of associations; it was a fundamental part of its political theory that "all le-

[29] James Hastings Nichols, *Democracy and the Churches* (Philadelphia, 1951), pp. 53–54.
[30] *Ibid.,* p. 84.

gitimate private societies have a just claim to protection by the State in the pursuit of all their proper ends" and that individuals "have a right to pursue their welfare . . . through mutual associations." [31] Leo XIII in the encyclical *Rerum Novarum* (1891) stated that the formation of such societies was a natural right of man, and that for the state to forbid the formation of private societies would be to contradict the principle of its own existence.[32]

No question of the right of association consequently existed, only the problem of adaptation to the practices and spirit of a parliamentary or democratic state. In one country after another, however, the local Catholics found it useful to organize politically along more democratic lines, as in Germany. Italian liberal Catholics eventually, with the formation of the Popolari, also adopted an affirmative approach. The discrediting of reactionary social elements by the end of the Second World War and the necessity of working with possible allies against the common danger of Communism added the final impulse to the transformation of Catholic parties into associations more in keeping with those of Wonderland.

Whatever their earlier pretensions may have been, the pressures of Wonderland gradually force the various associations into acknowledging the superior claims of the general welfare as well as adjusting their practices to the existence of other organizations. The ways in which groups in the United States have been so molded, even where parallel organizations in some other countries have not, is testimony to the American powers of absorption. It is a two-way process, on the one

[31] John A. Ryan and Francis J. Boland, *Catholic Principles of Politics* (New York, 1948), p. 131.
[32] *The Papal Encyclicals in their Historical Context,* edited by Anne Fremantle (New York, 1956), pp. 189–190.

hand frustration or punishment if nondemocratic methods are used, and on the other, the assurance of security, thereby ending the necessity for maintaining a powerful defensive structure. Over the years, the extremist visions fade into obscurity, are postponed to a distant future, or continue to be cherished by only a lunatic fringe of the membership, as a group, in the previously quoted words of William James, "inevitably meets with friction and opposition from its neighbors. In order to survive, it finds necessary the compromising of its original pretensions."

The intrusion of authoritarian regimes into the pattern of evolution also requires further comment. Judging strictly from the associational viewpoint, one can distinguish two more or less distinct sources for a modern dictatorship, the first stemming from the original conflict with traditional corporations at bay, while the second issues out of later failures to assimilate powerful associations, at least some of which have emerged out of the newly released forces. In the first instance, the older type of associations seek to maintain their positions as states within the state, to preserve all of their antiquated prerogatives in an era of change. The reforming elements, searching for means to remove their obstructive efforts, discover that no power in the community is strong enough to curb these major organizations except that of the state itself, and therefore an otherwise excessive statism is woven into their political ideology. In a populace not yet accustomed to the habits of internal cohesion despite the growth of national feeling, the state must exercise stringent control over associations in order to assure the domestic co-operation existing without coercion in the stable, democratic nations. In the course of grappling with the entrenched interests, dictatorial methods very probably are introduced. The less the time of transition from a medieval society to a modern, the more likely is an inflexible statism, as in Russia, which battens off the memories of former privileged groups and the assumption that any relaxation of central control would bring back older conditions.

The other occasion for dictatorship occurs later, after the apparent triumph of democracy, if too many powerful associations, perhaps including surviving representatives of the erstwhile corporations, have not been reconciled to democratic compromises. Dictatorship follows if the community proves unable to impose a consciousness of the common welfare or to bring them to function in accordance with the practices of the national family. Periods of crisis, economic or otherwise, may intensify irresponsible conduct. Wherever the associations imperil national cohesion, wherever they elevate their own welfare above that of the commonwealth, they place their own existence in jeopardy by stimulating a profound reaction in favor of the wholeness of the community. The state then ruthlessly crushes the more exaggerated pretensions of organized groups; if such a regime leaves memories of tyranny, it also bequeaths in the long run a more unified people, both from its own intense nationalistic propaganda and, conversely, from the common effort required by the subsequent struggle against its despotism.

Hence the assumption of total control by the state stands as a corrective, or punitive, result of the failure of an associational system. In the modern community, however, the dictatorship can be little more than a transitional force, inasmuch as the diverse multiplicity renders futile any attempt at a permanent integration of society on a monist basis. The concept of a general will, deprived of a plausibility perhaps acceptable in a simpler society, becomes increasingly a travesty on reality, and must now be artificially stimulated by the adrenaline of exaggerated nationalism or Marxism. On a less intense level, however, this same concept lies at the very basis of popular sovereignty. Thus the two tendencies, centripetal and centrifugal, oscillate back and forth in a pluralistic democracy, combining the best elements of both and providing a certain degree of healthy tension as they balance one another.

5
THE PERILOUS JOURNEY

And what of those nations, many of them newly independent, who lack the means and the experience for the successful implementation of the government of Wonderland? The question is an imperative one, for these peoples, from cultures that run the gamut of man's ascent from savagery to civilization, make up the majority of the planet's population. What of those who still face a long and perilous journey to Wonderland?

News of the emergent world of the future had been brought to the inhabitants of Africa and Asia during the great era of European imperialism. Such a preponderance of economic and technological strengths had been amassed by the burgeoning forces of Wonderland that their now comparatively paltry state powers crumbled as the radiating influences of an explosive West, swiftly assuming a political form, engulfed their homelands. The physical apparatus of a youthful world crowded in upon the ancient scene, soon to ignite the identical forces that had energized the West.

Even as these modern empires of coal and steel were reaching their brief apogee, the older, the traditional, empires collapsed, undermined by these same forces. Titles and dynasties, the kaisers of the world, whose names were of the very essence of the world preceding Wonderland, abruptly disappeared. Starting with the celestial emperor of China and ending with the shadowy figure of the Caliph of Islam, there finally vanished, in the dozen years centering on the First World War, the faintly lingering presence of the ages when they had been the enduring pillars of man's political abode. They were not so much overthrown as contemptuously discarded by a generation which in the act decisively turned its vision from the past to the future.

For peoples under colonial domination, European rule was the first phase, a transitory one, of the entrance into the future. The constant reminder, through the repeated glimpses of men and articles from Wonderland, of a higher plane of material existence, inspired imitation. Elements for their own dissolution, furthermore, had been carried within themselves by the invading empires through their principles of national independence, freedom of speech and press, and the usage of political associations for organized efforts. Once rebel voices were raised, the European imperial state was to a greater or lesser extent inhibited from employing age-old methods of repression by the ideological bases of its own existence; the emergence of political entities kindred, in spirit and practice, to itself, constrained a reluctant withdrawal as the vacuum was replaced by vital local forces.

Whatever the superficial appearance of insurrection against the West by these peoples, Wonderland was, in effect, fulfilling its own nature, following its own logical processes in their midst, by the struggle for independence. Despite the initial emotional impulse, the new countries, at least at first, did not secede from the West; they took a long step forward into it. As the empires gave way, nations cast in the Western mold sprang into being, together with the typical political life of an early stage of development. Shortly before the First World War the total number of sovereign countries was just over fifty; half a century later the roll call of the nations had more than doubled, and the list continued to lengthen. In many of these, with all due allowance for differences in local circumstances and traditions, one might anticipate a repetition in broad outline of the experiences of the Western countries in coming to terms with the new forces, the nineteenth century all over again in the twentieth, with Asiatic and African names and places.

A North American, in this connection, naturally thinks of his neighbors to the south and their long series of trials in implementing a government constitutionally more or less modeled on that of the United States. Only as they have built the social and economic foundations of the modern community do their political institutions assume a measure of true stability, whereas previous attempts at genuine republican government were inevitably followed by a relapse into another dictatorship. To this day, the success of each country is measured in rough proportion to such basic prerequisites as high literacy, the growth of a middle class, and the establishment of responsible associations.

A European might recall the equally optimistic adoption of parliamentary institutions in the new countries of Central Europe and the Balkans when they became independent. A type of government borrowed from that of Great Britain or

France quickly became, in most instances, a veneer for actual control by limited groups, such as the Court, the army officer corps, and the large landowners, because the ingredients for authentic political representation were not yet adequate. Ironically, the present generation, more likely to settle into a successful evolution, was to be denied the opportunity.

No longer, as a result of long and disillusioning experience, can one believe that the overthrow of a monarchy or a traditional type of government and the substitution of a constitution, parliament, and republic necessarily guarantees an actual advance, politically, into Wonderland. Methods of government cannot be imported and installed in the manner that railroads, airplanes, and modern factories are borrowed. Hammering together the structure of a republican system may represent a promise of progress but in itself is assuredly not the ultimate goal, for an autocratic regime or the despotism of a class can flourish equally successfully behind the facade of the new framework — for a time — as in the older. Political practices, regardless of forms, tend to follow the community direction of gravity, of seeking the common level of practices outside the political field. In the journey to Wonderland must occur a parallel development of the material and civic prerequisites for admission to modern citizenship; to the extent that these conditions remain unfulfilled, Wonderland's government, when attempted, will falter or fail. Whereas the more advanced countries can be expected to reveal a pattern of evolution in the mechanics and effectiveness of representation, those not yet internally prepared for these stages are likely to undergo a disillusioning cycle of brave new attempts at democratic government and subsequent relapses into less advanced political methods.

With each resurrection of democracy, a fresh start is made, and the goals of the perilous journey again emblazoned in the public imagination. Even though the apparatus of a pluralist democracy fails to function, a more simple form of republicanism at the least provides temporary political experience and precedents necessary for later advances. Nevertheless, if the bases for the complex institutions and practices have not yet been provided, the customary symptoms of deterioration soon become manifest. Politicians, not yet properly geared into any adequately functioning machinery of popular representation, tend to become a self-interested clique and an obstruction to the proper effectiveness of the state. Once again, as in the case of Italy at one time, the government increasingly displays the characteristics of an immature popular regime: the overemphasis on key personalities; usage of the government for personal gain, with ensuing corruption; a multi-party system not yet representing functional elements of the nation, and the consequent lack of any motivating drive beyond the vested interests of the politicians; and the persistent threat of nondemocratic groups.

If the nation lacks the skill to operate the machinery of modern politics, the bankrupt system presently goes into the receivership of another strong-man regime, often masquerading under a set of popular slogans and providing the functions of authority on a more rudimentary political level. Eventually a new struggle against tyranny opens the way for another attempt at democracy. Thus the process of political education and of constructive material development proceeds until a level finally is reached where, under conditions relatively salubrious for democratic institutions, there will evolve the more precise instruments of representation for the diverse elements of the community.

For some peoples who have only recently commenced the long journey, where the implements of Wonderland stand in stark contrast to everyday scenes reminiscent of ancient times, the goal seems painfully remote. Near an oil well camps a clan whose way of life remains much like that of their forefathers in the days of the Sabaeans. A concrete dam holds the water for irrigating fields tilled as they were when the Pharaohs ruled the land. Modern highways, laid out along the caravan routes of the Babylonians, carry busses past villages where oxen pull the carts. Or an even more dramatic contrast, an African witch doctor, still articulating the vestiges of the long-submerged Neolithic, plies his trade a few miles from a modern hospital.

If the elements of the community are heaped together in such incongruity to one another, the hitherto dormant political forces, when activated, are likely to be equally disharmonious. The coming of Wonderland, in these regions, with the consequent telescoping of history, brings into juxtaposition social phenomena which have hitherto been unrelated. Groups representative of different eras, social and political outlooks and techniques from widely disparate historical periods, function side by side in the same national community; on paper at least, they abruptly find themselves operating according to forms of government which took centuries to develop and which require several generations of practice before becoming habitual and natural.

For the historian, mob scenes in the Arabic world evoke a sense of familiarity, as though he had stepped back to ancient Alexandria or Antioch and were witnessing one of their frequent street brawls. At such a moment, the telescoping of history may strike him with such intense reality that he fancies Ptolemaic Egypt or Seleucid Syria to have adopted the political organs of a modern democracy, complete with president, parliament, and cabinet system. While such an innovation would obviously have had no possibility of success, many twentieth-century countries have inaugurated their independence burdened by a society in which at least three-fourths of the population is no more ready for modern citizenship than two thousand years ago. For the bulk of those abruptly invested with modern citizenship, material conditions have not changed markedly in the meantime, and a measure of the immense distance which remains to be traversed is graphically visible in the repeated manifestations of politics at their most rudimentary.

Far removed from the theoretical frame of reference of political science, government is then reduced to the elemental task of maintaining order among a people who, newly escaped from centuries of despotism, are still apt to carry with them a deeply engraved animus against any superior authority. A benevolent regime which allows freedom to act and speak is, for many brought up in the atmosphere of absolutism, a weak regime, scorned by the most restless and vocal elements. This attitude, so far from the concepts of Western politics, is conveyed, for instance, in the sardonic comment, quoted by Gibb and Bowen, about one of the governors of Damascus during the Ottoman Empire: "Abd el-Ra'ûf Pasha was mild, just, and peace-loving, and because of his exceeding justice the people of Damascus were emboldened against him." [1]

Probably the fairest, and soundest, *point d'appui* for an understanding of the new republics' position is that, for the time being, they function amidst a medley of circumstances not very dissimilar from the republican city-state in ancient or medieval times. Where a number of groups were in a position to grasp for power in one of these, a succession of gaudy political explosions enliven their chronicles, while the more stable republics were those in which a group or interlocking groups had achieved a permanent oligarchic control.

In any given year in the new republics, without considering the momentum of change, the situation seems potential with

[1] Hamilton Gibb and Harold Bowen, *Islamic Society and the West,* p. 205.

oligarchic rule. Old-fashioned despotism is swept away, but the public concept of the state is still far removed from acceptance of equitable representation for all groups or of a peaceful equilibrium among them. Each ambitious group seeks to control the levers of political power for itself, and, if successful, the personnel and powers of the new ruling groups soon blur into the machinery of the state itself. The leaders quickly assume the psychology of the officials in the overthrown state, the habitual attitudes and conduct being carried over into the new dispensation. The equation of government with *strong* rule, the sword as a valid sceptre, authority vested in those best fitted to rule, intolerance of organizations not directly linked to the state — these ideas are likely to characterize both the old and the new regimes.

Perhaps this political world can be most succinctly summed up by recalling Vilfredo Pareto's dictum of history as the cemetery of aristocracies, a world wherein a group with a lust for power seized the state by intrigue and brute force, which maintained hegemony by combining terror with a calculated usage of man's irrational moods, and which eventually paid for gaining the virtues of civilization by losing power. This is the jungle of politics, one from which our ancestors escaped, which is slowly being tamed by the advance of Wonderland's government. Even though the compulsions to oligarchy master any given group, the same forces which overthrew the kaisers and evicted the European colonial masters surge inexorably against any new attempt to set up a permanent authority over the populace.

II

Basically, the problem of governing many of these countries comes down to dealing with two contrasting sets of circumstances, the one dictating the strong-arm methods which alone can restrain chaotic disorder, while the other contains elements as ready for authentic democracy as any in Wonderland. Pareto's world still exercises its permeating gravitation, and yet, increasingly, statecraft must pay obeisance to a higher level.

Most fortunate is a newly independent people where the prestige of a democratic, national party, which led the campaign for freedom, permits the inauguration of a stable government on a high level. The peaceful acquisition of independence within the Commonwealth of Nations, for example, has provided an auspicious introduction to self-government through the utilization of genuine parliamentary institutions and ministerial responsibility. Such a party, countrywide in scope and rooted among the more vocal elements, profits from the initial impetus of national feeling and sense of unity achieved during the struggle for national freedom. Its guardianship permits the original leaders to guide affairs during the formative years while a more durable stability comes into being and the mold is set for the habitual political life of the community. However unhealthy a one-party preponderance for a more advanced country, in new nations it is so common a phenomenon as to be characteristic; at the *outset,* it is probably beneficial that the politically active, who flock into the party, should learn to work together while also providing some measure of representation for the various elements within the nation.

That even some Commonwealth countries have been unable to maintain a genuine parliamentary government for any length of time provides one indication of the prevailing weaknesses in the new states. Those less fortunate, such as a people only liberated through years of violent struggle, are likely to suffer a later period of continued internal violence or the painful antidote of an oppressive dictatorship. Nor does the use of force necessarily bear the moral stigma that it has in Wonderland. The spectacle of elections bought or coerced and of politicians operating a racket, so often the case in this early stage of development, obviously confers no moral ascendancy upon the democratic processes. Quite the contrary, they may be regarded as merely methods giving an unfair advantage to certain interests — the sword may seem the cleaner.

A potential source for violence is also to be found in the nature of those organized groups that have come into existence. In most instances the membership is no more prepared to practice democratic procedures within the group than in their national government; because the number of individuals able to play a proper role in the modern association is proportionately much lower than in Wonderland, a rigid control over the rank and file must be exercised by the inner circle. In order to maintain leadership over this mass following, methods closer to its common denominator must be employed, the most effective being appeals to the strongest emotions. Hence, the leaders, in using the organization for their own purposes, are committed, by the nature of their tool, to a crudeness of action that they might privately deplore, while in other instances the nature of the following will throw into leadership those who are themselves the most apt exponents of these methods. Even though the superficial structure may approach that of the modern association, the spirit and mode of conduct are likely to partake more nearly of tribal traditions, of the military, or even of the medieval religious sect.

The absence of the safeguards of an associational equilibrium sharpens the instincts of self-preservation in the existent organized social groups. Its members lacking a sense of mature nationhood, each is more conscious of its own goals and of the iniquities of rivals than of the traits held in common or of the welfare of the whole community. Antagonisms among groups, some defending long held positions and others fighting for a greater role, place a premium upon discipline of membership, a militant leadership, and methods other than democratic.

Also characteristic at this time, when a people's social organization may still be primarily tribal, is the relative paucity of major associations, which in turn gives an otherwise undue prominence to those that do exist. Herein lies the possibility that a group which possesses a strategic location within society or holds potent weapons, placed in its hands by the community, may sooner or later use its advantages to strike for the emoluments and privileges of supreme authority. During the transition to Wonderland, before a restraining balance of power has been established, one strategic group may find the road to power alluringly open to itself.

Where a nation spawns violent groups, the military holds trumps, that is, it possesses what normally must be accounted the ultimate weapon of decision. Hence army officers have played a role out of all proportion to their numbers or intrinsic importance in countries not yet in the final stages of evolution. Very often, they become the depository of power through the bankruptcy of leadership or paralysis of civilian authorities, and they then institute the typical strong arm regime of a nation unable to govern itself. In recent years, however, the comparatively well educated officers of the armed forces, especially in countries that seem within reach of stable civilian control, have sometimes shown a tendency to serve as guardians of democracy, that is, forcibly liquidating a dictatorial regime and then presiding over an attempted renewal of popularly elected government.

The increasing urgency of the march to Wonderland may, perhaps, prove to have the effect of disrupting the cycle of popular government and strong man rule in immature countries. With the old-fashioned despotism, and its reliance on tradition backed by police power, as extinct as the static society which it governed, the circumstances in politically immature countries are potential with a different type of despotism. A dictatorial regime must now learn to control an increasingly dynamic, increasingly restive, populace. Not even the most devoted and competent believer in a Western style of democracy is likely to find possible the full implementation of his beliefs, inasmuch as he must deal with existent forces, work with available human tools, and act within the social and economic framework of his own community. The pressure to shore up the regime by nondemocratic methods incessantly play upon the men in office: the dangers of counter-revolution from challenged traditional corporations or vested interests; the equal menace from emergent organizations conditioned by their own environment to violence and unrestrained by a balance of power; real or fancied threats of aggression from neighboring nations, which entails the maintenance of national unity; the necessity of imposing internal nationhood upon a people still lacking the unifying Western network of voluntary associations. Under conditions where outbreaks of violence are likely, the inner logic of statecraft drives the ruling group to the employment of political techniques which within the context of Wonderland are assumed to be evil.

For the statesman in one of these countries, the political realities which determine his pragmatic manipulation of the social forces in his community are quite as tangible and even more imperative than the economic problems. Operating on a civic level where politics is still primarily a matter of personalities, he can hardly avoid employing the myth of the Great Man, it being the most effective means for bringing popular sentiment to a focus. Legitimacy having vanished in revolution, and men's minds requiring its tranquilizing reappearance, symbols and slogans appropriate to the new authority must be indelibly engraved in the consciousness of the citizens through intensive propaganda campaigns. Crusades must be launched against the enemy, who, depending upon momentary circumstances, may be found in the old colonial master, a neighboring state, or an internal villain, such as an older vested interest or an unpopular minority group.

Announced objectives of the government are not necessarily substantive in the sense of actually motivating the actions of a regime. They are used simply as functional tools for keeping the most vocal elements occupied while presumably more constructive growth takes place; that is, an elite or oligarchy with its own position in jeopardy almost automatically develops techniques of statecraft partaking of an esoteric nature. While knowing full well, within the confines of the group, that their methods are only devices for manipulating the populace, their overt actions descend to the low level of the most vocal elements in its organized manifestations, and the public policy *verbally* reflects the popular shibboleths. In the process, the spirit of politics, though not necessarily the specific details, has reverted to that of Pareto's world. Quite aside from the obvious effect of debasing rather than elevating the political level of a people, the usage of politics of this kind risks the possibility that the regime will lose control of the situation; that is, trapped by its own devices, it may become a prisoner of the forces evoked. Caught in a *cul-de-sac,* the leaders may be driven to reckless adventure, disastrous to the nation and a peril to the international society of nations.

Some of these techniques, and others like them, are as old as the politics described by Pareto, and they form, to some degree, an integral part of politics also in the most advanced nations. Their usage varies according to local traditions of politics, the circumstances within the country, and the nature of the temporarily dominant group or groups. Where national leaders succumb to the temptation to entrench themselves permanently in a monopoly of power, they must inevitably intensify and systematize these practices, while also invoking public discipline on behalf of a march to a Wonderland of their own naming. Whether this latter form of despotism, exemplified by the Communist party, can, by channelizing the forces leading to Wonderland, survive with much greater tenacity than simple strong man rule has scarcely been proven yet. For the time being, however, the resources of the community are increasingly allocated to the maintenance of the political establishment itself, and the journey of the peasant is correspondingly deflected into the wilderness.

III

For the citizen of Wonderland, the presence of the Communist party in this century has constituted an exasperating intrusion into the anticipated sequence of progressive development. Inexplicable from the viewpoint of the modern community, the party nonetheless is comprehensible as a possible derivative out of the circumstances of the perilous journey. Though obviously the appearance of this particular organization was far from inevitable, the broad circumstances were and are potential with a major historical phenomenon of such a nature; this area has been pre-empted by the massive power structure of Communism, but had this not happened, its place would almost certainly have been taken by organizations of the same general species, though not, of course, with precisely the same doctrines or forms.

A development somewhat on the order of a mutation occurred in Russia when an association, fundamentally Western in origins, unexpectedly proved effective in a very different milieu, in a largely underdeveloped country in the early stages of the transition to Wonderland. An organization originally forged, in its apparatus and techniques, for the intense rivalry of associations in an advanced community vaulted into power in a very different situation and became the prisoner of forces leading to oligarchy. It need not have occurred in Russia — it surely would not, without the First World War and the adamant will power of Lenin — but here existed a set of circumstances, subsequently typical of many other countries, wherein this type of denouement could happen.

From the original Marxist Socialist movement of western Europe the Russian Communists inherited the structure and procedures of the western association. Here had been imprinted such elements as the terminology of the working class movement and that intensely vivid insight into the associational level within the national community which is sometimes so devastatingly perceptive and often, now, so obviously old-fashioned. The original Marxist doctrines appeared as definitive enunciations of a complex process still in too early a stage of evolution for accurate observation or description. Marx caught a glimpse of the constant competition and tension between groups and proceeded to magnify one aspect of it out of all proportions to its true place. The pressures, the aggressive group qualities, existed, but to call the resultant rivalries a "class struggle" was to make a caricature of the whole process. Clinging to its author and animating the universalizing of group ideas was the residue of the spirit engendered by the older all-inclusive guild or corporation and the presence of an oppressing, privileged oligarchy.

According to the naive dreams of the early Social Democrats, an advancing industrial society would inevitably pass under the hegemony of the working classes. Instead, most of the socialists eventually conformed to the pressures of Wonderland, their organizations accommodating themselves to parliamentary practices and the domestic balance of power. That country in which the full vigor of the original revolutionary party was successful was one least expected, one with an industrial development far below the level presumed necessary for a socialist victory. It was a triumph originally as bewildering to the Marxists themselves as to others.

Lenin, in deliberately adapting the Bolsheviks to specifically Russian conditions, perfected an instrument for incessant political and social struggle in a nondemocratic situation. Communism, molded by that governmental violence which had long begat nihilistic counter-violence, carried to the logical extreme the concept of warfare within the nation. The Communists were prepared to use whatever methods worked, physical violence or otherwise, in order to achieve victory: organizing themselves like a military force, subject to strict obedience to the leaders; fighting for control of any segment of national life or sources of power as though they were geographical military objectives; using any tactics or strategy without any consideration for normal standards of human life; the confiscation of enemy property; the ruthless slaughtering of domestic enemies as though they were opponents on the battlefield. The effect was like a professional army invading and conquering civilians who had little comprehension, at first, that they were involved in a war at all. In a more stable and properly organized community this reckless extremism would have generated massive opposition on an organizational basis and such methods would have stultified themselves. Here, however, the traditional government had only been newly swept away and the growing network of associations had not yet become sufficiently integrated or stabilized to restrain the outlaw group.

In the Russian Communists the working class movement found, in name at least, its self-centered and dogmatic quintessence, its most concentrated form. As a group which has achieved its wildest dreams and actually possesses the physical power to mold the community in its own image, the Communist party represents, furthermore, the most extreme form of the association. Transposing the spirit and methods of the mobilized nation at war to lesser social entities, it embodies within itself the most intense rivalries of modern society. The Communist party is to associational rivalries what the strongly militarized nation is to the struggle for survival in an age of exaggerated nationalism. Lenin's creation of the revolutionary party is parallel to that of Hitler on the national level, both possessing the advantages and liabilities of such intensity of organization.

To this day, the Soviet government has retained, in its procedures and forms, an appearance alien and yet oddly familiar to the Western observer. That which is familiar is the associational structure and spirit, definitely related to the local societies among which we live, but which has been projected upon a gigantic scale. Within the Communist association, now primarily representative of the Russian so-called intelligentsia, ambitious individuals climb the hierarchy by a process of personal politics and attainment of positions of strength not dissimilar from that in Western groups. A self-perpetuating clique at the top manipulates the machinery of the party, and the ratification of decisions reached by these leaders is as much a formality as is usually the case in American conventions. Clusters of committees here also serve as the working bodies for the party as a whole. (In 1917 a committee was appointed to carry through the Petrograd revolution, and, when successful, the chairman composed a report!) Differences of opinion must be threshed out — sometimes vociferously — behind closed doors, and an external appearance of unity maintained. Despite the absolutism of the party, it has persisted in going through the ritual of congresses, of speeches and voting, the procedure of a major democratic association in the West.

Although these external features have remained, the fundamental character of the party underwent a further transformation once the group, as rulers, was fully subject to the pressures of Russian circumstances. A political association, having assumed the place of the traditional aristocracy in order to impose the dictatorship of the proletariat, was itself subtly molded by influences inherent in the position of Russian leadership into a rough copy of those they had ousted. The Communist party responded to the circumstances and pressures of Pareto's world by becoming a new oligarchy, until, under Stalin, the contours of the Tsar's regime all too clearly reasserted themselves. An oligarchy which in other ages and places could be based on mercantile or landowning or religious elements was here, through the telescoping of history, mustered in modern associational array, though its driving spirit was that of armed warriors on horseback.

In many ways the party took on the characteristics of politics in underdeveloped countries during the age of transition, and as such it possesses distinct advantages in those nations. In part, of course, these rise out of its insistent offers to lead a successful march to Wonderland. More immediately decisive, however, and one not always sufficiently comprehended in advanced communities, is the advantage of organizational efficiency, and here, rather than in economics, can be the key factor in countries lacking a network of established groups. In an associational age, the Communists are able, in any given country, to establish quickly this vital element and thereby gain an initial strategic opportunity. They can rapidly reproduce the popular manifestations of a democracy by means of a functioning political party, a strong leadership, and, most important, a national network of local groups, while, with a well-stocked arsenal of techniques, the party members need not learn by trial and error the patterns of political behavior. In the prevailing absence of other strong associations when a traditional despotism is destroyed, or in the first months after the overthrow of a dictatorship before other political groups are properly established, it has a particular advantage. Its proffer of mass support to a wobbly revolutionary regime can be very tempting, and the threatened blackmail of anti-regime riots may be equally persuasive.

Their activity highlights the increasing importance of another major development in this century, not new, but quite likely to grow in scope as conditions encourage it. The seeding of local Communist groups in all countries, carefully nourishing them to the optimum strength possible under prevalent conditions there, and then, when feasible, using them to extend the Communist empire — this has become the pattern of what might be called an *associational imperialism*. The evolution of international machinery and the massing of opinion against the employment of military aggression for purposes of territorial expansion puts increasing emphasis on other means of aggrandizement, and its inborn propensity to regard the association, rather than the nation, as the paramount social unit, gives the Communist party an opportunity to profit by this situation. Nor are the Communists the only ones to have practised this technique of conquest; still vividly familiar is its usage by the Nazis through their local parties in the Saar, Danzig, Austria, the Sudetenland, and other regions.

One might, in fact, go one step further and see in the international politics of this century the challenge of the would-be oligarchies, ostensibly based on race or class, seeking to assert control of the planet over those states which are based upon a pluralist society. Habituated to their own mode of maintaining political monopoly and perhaps unconsciously confessing the nature of their own methods, they persist in interpreting conditions in the pluralist communities in terms of domination by some group. Subjected to natural pressures for greater freedom from elements in their own population, the elite must mount a permanent offensive, they must create, for their system, the impression of an overwhelmingly successful momentum. Thus the democracies, which emerged out of the unseating, usually, of privileged, hereditary aristocracies, must now resume the long struggle for survival against new elites in countries where circumstances encourage their growth. Seen in this perspective, the planetary panorama can be depicted in terms of a struggle to determine which type of government is best suited to the age, the monopoly of the state by one politically oriented group or the political equilibrium of the many groups.

While the Communists have thought to find promising opportunities in underdeveloped countries, a very different type of problem has increasingly confronted the party in its original homeland: namely, what happens when the perilous journey of the peasant approaches its material goal? How does a nation which is achieving the material progress required for Wonderland now break out of methods progressively more obstructive to genuine progress? In Marxist phraseology, by what process does the promised withering away of the state come to pass?

Though Russia may have been backward in many respects in 1917, its accelerating momentum of progress before the war had already created rather large, though poorly organized, enclaves of Wonderland. The new masters struck down all possible organizational competitors in their original attainment of power and thereafter remained jealously intolerant of any possible rivals. The long duration of the harsh reign of terror is a measure of the intrinsic strength of those natural tendencies which the oligarchy sought to extinguish. In their continuing presence, unorganized and repressed as they were, lay the reason for the seeming inability of the Communists to terminate their cycle of revolution; that is, these methods were encouraged by the abiding fear that the cessation of terror would see an irretrievable breakthrough of the forces antithetical to the original purposes of the party.

In the Soviet Union, with its tyranny of one association over the people, an immense weight of controls has been imposed to prevent that which is accepted as natural and desirable in advanced nations. If those agencies which are a very important part of the machinery whereby the nation expresses itself are throttled, the vitality of the social forces of the nation is mortally damaged. Taine described, in the last century, the circumstances wherein the state "kills or paralyzes these natural organizations or prevents their birth; and hence so many precious organs, which, absorbed, atrophic or abortive, are lost to the great social body." [2] Where the state has total control over the associations, he wrote, "the community consists only of automata manouevered from above, infinitely small residues of men, passive, mutilated, and, so to say, dead souls. . . ." [3] Another Frenchman, Jean Bodin, had asserted substantially the same thing back in the sixteenth century: "If you eliminate corporate groups and communes you will ruin the commonwealth and you will change it into a barbarous tyranny." [4]

These quotations could have been penned as an exact description of Stalinist Russia. Nevertheless, by the very act of building the material circumstances for Wonderland, the ruling group in the long run has nourished the growing potential of other associational elements. Chaotic forces continue to seek organization; in every segment of the vast economy ambitious men seek means for enhancing their projects and personal fortunes, and men of similar interests

[2] Hippolyte A. Taine, *The Modern Regime,* Vol. I, p. 120.
[3] *Ibid.,* p. 116.
[4] Quoted in Dietrich Gerhard, "Periodization in European History," *The American Historical Review,* LXI (July, 1956), p. 909.

inevitably drift into spontaneous contacts and alliances and unofficial co-operation. Beneath the level of forbidden formal organization, the shapes of shadowy association take on tangibility. Their sum total becomes a massively permeating pressure against the restraints of the oligarchy.

This is the crux of the matter, the very core of reality in the twentieth-century evolution into Wonderland. The observer cannot help but feel that he is seeing an elemental, unconquerable movement at work which, however much balked at any given moment, soon resumes its course like a mighty stream finding its way around and over all obstacles. Its power of relentless erosion will eventually wear down any artificial structure erected to block its course. A dictatorship or would-be oligarchy which throws itself athwart this movement speedily finds itself at war with the very nature of the modern, pluralistic community. For a time, the normal evolution of society, in rough response to the natural forces of the age, is paralyzed. Large and vital elements, frustrated in their natural development, generate terrible tensions within the community. In the fascist states, this forced ever more rigid controls, which only worsened the maladjustments until the vicious cycle was resolved by military adventure. The ultimate upshot of such a dilemma is either release in an external direction, that is, by war, or else the facing of the consequences internally, a readjustment in a direction giving relief to these pressures. Nikita Khrushchev, the heir of Stalin, tried to carry on the momentum of Communist expansion, and, failing this, was obliged to seek internal changes to relieve the pressure.

To quote chapter and verse on associational tendencies within a dictatorship and its obscuring censorship is virtually impossible. Nevertheless, such a qualified observer as Alexander Vucinich asserts that unofficial groups are constantly tending to appear and that the legal organizations persistently

attempt to veer off on their own natural tangents.[5] Klaus
Mehnert believes that the Russian is predisposed to col-
lectivism in the form of associations "naturally developed,
spontaneous, unorganized, and unplanned"; where they do
appear, they are branded as "unhealthy" manifestations.[6]
The very persistence of the press in belaboring associational
feelings outside of state and party is indirect evidence of
their existence.

When Khrushchev admitted the deficiencies of the mono-
lithic bureaucratic state by his territorial decentralization
of the economy, one could suspect that he was responding,
in part, to the natural pressures of a pluralistic community.
Though his solution was deliberately intended to gain the
advantages of relatively autonomous initiative without unleashing associational forces, the new framework would almost
certainly have eased the way for their further growth. Infinitely revealing was the indirect admission of associational
pressures in Khrushchev's statement to the 1959 Congress
of the party that the time was not yet ripe for organizations
to take over in the Soviet Union. In another Congress, two
years later, he found it necessary to promise that the role of
associations would be enlarged in future years. The actions
of the Yugoslav regime, forced to reach compromises with
forces indigenous to the country, were surely foreshadowing
the route that the Soviet oligarchy must eventually follow.

In the final analysis, it is the transitoriness of that phenomenon which made possible the existence of the Communist regime, the telescoping of history that would seem
to ensure the eventual liquidation of the oligarchy. Socialist
principles which in the West were to a greater degree based

---

[5] Alexander Vucinich, *Soviet Economic Institutions: The Social Structure of Production Units* (Stanford, 1953), pp. 43–44, 46–50.
[6] Klaus Mehnert, *Der Sowjetmensch*, 6th ed. (Stuttgart, 1959),
p. 301, 415.

on observed data, which were relatively plastic to reality and subject to discussion and modification, in Russia became rigid dogma. In part the consequences of an embattled garrison status where ideas serve as weapons, the Russian Communist mentality had also reflected the psychology of the static community in which the Russian thinkers of the preceding century had conceived their visions of the future. Its intellectual tools inadequate for comprehending the full nature of the modern society, Communist thought has long since assumed a dated appearance, the expressed ideas conveying a sense of being out of joint with the times. Under its domination, Russian society has retained a nineteenth-century flavor, as though every facet of life except the industrial economy were suffering from arrested development.

Its thought processes, dominated by absolutes, are fundamentally incapable of recognizing the multiplicity in Wonderland, and, limited in its perception of change to the rudimentary Hegelian concept, the Communist mind cannot comprehend the Western metamorphosis into something very different from the days of Karl Marx. In its rigid dichotomy, the ever-changing contours and forces of the West must still be labelled as bourgeois and capitalist. Lenin, in the Russian Revolution, wanted to skip capitalism and go directly to socialism. America, that land which rouses in the Russian such mingled fascination and repulsion, is skipping socialism and has entered, by a process of natural evolution, into a new type of society which achieves the ultimate material goals that the socialists desire, and which has grown beyond the old bourgeois state into a Wonderland whose associations represent the entire community.

Hope has never been completely abandoned that the Communist party would eventually follow the course of other associations into a voluntaristic, democratic mode. In Wonderland the Communist parties have encountered the by now virtually instinctive reaction to recalcitrant groups, that is, drawing them into the community of fellowship through conciliation when they behave according to the prevailing norms, and hurling them into the outer darkness of public obloquy when they relapse into more crude practices. Repeatedly rejecting the opportunity to join the fraternity of free associations, the party was itself rejected, its membership depleted and devitalized by the digestive processes of democratic public opinion.

On the international level, the nations of Wonderland have operated in essentially the same way. The lost gamble of the Americans at the end of the Second World War to remove the suspicions of the Russians by concessions, was motivated, primarily, by an attempt to assimilate them to the practices of Wonderland. Failing in this, the West responded by the process of containment in order to ensure that violent methods would not succeed. When the Communists gave some indications of abandoning these methods, hopes were once again aroused that at long last the Russian Communists were discovering the usefulness of adhering to the norms of Wonderland and that Western methods, adopted as expedients, would in time become habitual. From frequent disillusionment deeply cynical of any conversion, the West could nevertheless hope that post-Stalinist Communism, which was being forced, in the Soviet Union, to grudging acknowledgment of the hard realities in foreign affairs and to a groping search for other solutions internally, might be the preliminary sign of the coming of the inevitable — the political acceptance of the idea of a pluralist community.

6

THE INSTITUTIONAL
DRIVE

On the perilous journey the populace may overthrow a tyranny, slaughter its agents and smash the symbols, only to see the same terror-instilling apparition later re-emerge under another name. At such times the migrant to Wonderland might sense, deeply imbedded in the processes of government, the existence of a fundamental force as intangible but apparently as inescapable as the law of gravity itself. An individual who migrates directly to an already established Wonderland also may be perturbed at seeing the increasing powers of government, and surmise it to be an augury of a despotism like that he had fled; here, too, even as the peasant settles in the modern community, could be detected the shadowy presence of the ancient oppressor.

While many factors are involved in the persistent curbing of human liberties, one element in the causality, a group of tendencies arising out of the needs of social organization, is increasingly spotlighted by circumstances especially characteristic of the twentieth-century society, a phenomenon here postulated under the name of the *institutional drive*. In sum, this refers to the tendency of any organization, associational or state, to intensify control over its membership while also reaching outward to strengthen its position in the environment. Originating as rational responses to problems of internal administration and external growth, the institutional drive develops an inner logic and autonomous momentum, if unchecked, which, taking primacy over the original purposes, elevates the pursuit of power itself into the supreme goal. It then functions in the community as a force in itself, pragmatic considerations of organizational welfare serving as a virtually exclusive center of gravity for its action. Inherent in any situation where men are joined in group enterprises, it is a sociological phenomenon both necessary and dangerous.

An American Conservative would find the term useful in expressing his conception of the growth of federal power in the United States. Others may immediately think of particular associations whose increasing control over spheres of community life arouses their antipathy. In actual truth, the institutional drive is, to a greater or lesser degree, an integral part of all social organization. Even on the most minute scale, in the local societies and clubs, a certain machine-like character becomes evident as successive officeholders step into an apparatus equipped with rules and cherished procedures created by the cumulative experiences of their predecessors. The organization has become a more or less automatically functioning entity, assured of sustained vitality by proven devices for securing recruits and for eliciting the co-operation of the membership.

In a major association of national size, the structure and procedures begin to assume institutional qualities. The vastly larger numbers, an inevitable loss of personal contact, the scale of activities, entail the maintenance of a governing nucleus to serve as the custodian of enterprises essential for associational welfare. Ostensibly, the nucleus merely reflects the will of the total membership; in actual practice, it never does function as a passive vehicle for the generality, inasmuch as administrative necessities very quickly assume preponderance in the thoughts, values, and actions of the officials. Inevitably, the leaders begin to feel themselves servants of the organization, rather than of the individual members. Preoccupied with its own particular set of problems, the nucleus generates a dynamic force within itself and tends to initiate a direction of development characteristic of all governing bodies and leading to internal control and external expansion. With increased efficiency and augmented power taking priority over the well-being of the followers, these men thus become the wielders of a more intensified institutional drive. Then, as the leaders, animated by administrative exigencies, seek to impose their own values upon the rank and file, as they equate the welfare of the whole association with the successes of officialdom, they veer increasingly away from authentic representation of the primary forces formally expressed by the organization.

Those who establish an organization or set up a new bureau in a government do more than inaugurate a new program; they bring into being a social organism with a vitality of its own. It sinks roots into the environment, seeking sustenance, more money and personnel, from the community. The men who have colonized in such an organization or bureau are henceforth dependent upon it for their livelihood and for the fulfillment of their ambitions. Like a farmer homesteading land or a businessman opening up a new economic enterprise, the official has found, in the social and political realm, an area wherein his labors may earn him advancement, and these energies, in turn, help to generate the institutional drive.

Within an organization intensely possessive of terrain already dominated and greedy for more, the drive manifests itself in a growing pattern of self-motivating and egocentric expansion. The words of Peter Viereck concerning intense nationalism could be applied to the more extreme instances found in fascist and communist groups:

> A pure force is completely self-determined. Its only righteousness is its self-fulfillment. Its only wrong is its compromise or frustration. It no more obeys the laws of morality than those of Euclid. Under the spell of pride, hate, and demagogy, it sweeps away like burst chains all laws outside itself. . . .[1]

As for associations in general, the goal of their dynamic force is likely to be the attainment of a status equivalent to that of a public institution: legal sanction for privileges and for the right of self-legislation, the transformation of the association into an involuntary group wherein the members are subject to the will of the governing clique, and an assured place for the leaders in the councils of the nation — an approximation, incidentally, of the position of the late medieval corporation. Once the organization is closely affiliated with the state, this phenomenon henceforth manifests itself primarily as a conservative force, intent on hoarding its privileges and snuffing out any incipient rivals or internal rebellion.

Helping to determine the vigor and success of the institutional drive of any given association are many factors, both internal and external. The internal strength is determined by such considerations as the resources already available to it

---

[1] Peter Viereck, *Conservatism Revisited: The Revolt Against Revolt, 1815–1949* (New York, 1950), p. 49.

in the number of members and their positions in the community, the competency of its leadership, the efficacy of such weapons as it may possess, the strictness of discipline over the members, and the persuasiveness of a sense of collective self-preservation in animating the conduct of those members. However potent any drive in itself may be, however, it obviously does not function in isolation or absolute freedom, its vigor being determined to some extent, and its success to a larger degree, by the interaction with its surroundings.

One would be tempted to suggest that the sketch of any idealized institutional drive would bear about as much resemblance to its actual tangible appearance in its environment as the economic laws of supply and demand do to their manifestations in the market. The opportunities for expansion are limited by many obstacles, including the restrictive power of the state itself and the pressures emanating from the drives of other associations. Out of the very multiplicity of vigorously growing social groups, as we already know, have evolved safeguards against its more extreme manifestations, particularly the equilibrium which checks the flagrant ambitions or violations of democratic procedures in any one of them. Equally salutary is the complex network of personal affiliations wherein any one individual distributes his interests and allegiances among numerous groups and thereby reduces his vulnerability to coercive tactics by any one of them.

Two external circumstances are especially stimulating for the drive, the one being the existence of conditions which enable the rapid physical growth of the organization, for example, an especially rapidly growing industry for the labor union concerned. The other, which forms a major theme in these pages, is the presence, real or assumed, of serious danger to a group. As noted earlier, associations in underdeveloped countries frequently feel the necessity for a centralization and aggressiveness which would not be condoned within the community of Wonderland.

One may assess the vital significance of the latter factor in determining the intensity of the drive — and see the contrast between Wonderland and the older order — by observing the behavior of minorities in the two environments. A genuine minority must maintain complete unity in order to balance the majority, nor can it compromise, for to do so would blur its front and thereby weaken it.[2] The power must be effectively mobilized by men possessing full rights of command, while the organization constantly maintains a belligerent stance against outsiders and surrounds its principles and symbols with the quality of sacrosanct dogma. Conditions of the old order, hence, spur the members themselves to ensure their own safety through the greatest possible fulfillment of the drive. In countries where traditions of violence remain strong and bitter rivalries prevail, the institutional drive (if the association survives at all) is thus much more likely to achieve its ultimate goal of an institutional status. Any association, minority or not, involved in a long and desperate struggle will almost automatically move in the direction of centralization. Under these conditions, the structure will necessarily tend to approximate the military prototype of the army, an organization created specifically for warfare, and which cannot function effectively or win victories unless it conforms to this pattern.

By contrast, the American associations live within the security provided by the associational equilibrium. The growth of social organizations is regarded as an essentially healthy development, and the initial phases of the institutional drive recognized as legitimate means for ensuring adequate repre-

---

[2] Georg Simmel, *Conflict,* translated by Kurt H. Wolff (Glencoe, Ill., 1955), p. 97.

sentation. When the momentum of a drive carries it beyond this practical need, however, resistance, both internal and external, is likely to mount against its further intensification. Since frenetic appeals to their survival as a group or demagogic maledictions upon purported enemies ring false in an atmosphere of general security, the leaders will presently be obliged to relax an unduly aggressive stance. A condition of security drains away the more immoderate pressures. Wonderland is a community which, through its rivalries, hones sharp the tools of an association and yet limits their usage to nonviolent methods.

From a statistical point of view, all organized groups are minorities within the complex American society. Throughout the history of the American republic there have always been instances of groups (immigrant, racial, economic, religious) which, for a time, displayed symptoms of a minority psychology. Any one of these has made a very uncomfortable neighbor for others, with its strident clamor and irrational egocentrism, its inability to recognize justice or sincerity in other points of view, and its ignorance or disregard of ethical behavior when its position was in question. Nevertheless, while one constantly glimpses aberrant tendencies striving to escape the restraining channels of community practices, in nearly all cases the achievement of equality and security, the assurance of a permanent place in the fraternity of associations, results in its assimilation to the prevailing norms. Those practices which are now typical of the American Wonderland, in fact, to a very considerable degree evolved out of the continuing experience in absorbing such groups.

In Wonderland the liberty of the individual is safeguarded as the various interests compete without resort to violence or crushing the individuals by jostling among these groups. Rivalries are fought out, above all, by means of a highly developed art of verbal persuasion, and no citizen can escape the constant demands of these groups for his allegiance, vote, money, or time. Since an organization dies without the energies of the individual, he must be induced, if he cannot be compelled, to harness his dedicated labors on behalf of its program. Many and ingenious are the devices for extracting his co-operation, not least the spirit-quailing moral pressures which the zealous, convinced spokesmen for any organization may bring to bear. The average citizen is the prey of many institutional drives, and the stronger the drive, the more his services tend to be expected as a matter of course.

The immigrant to Wonderland, or its native-born citizen, who daily is flicked by the sting of brusque requests for compliance as he is importuned, lectured, threatened, or cajoled, could find in the concept of the institutional drive an invaluable tool. It is a concept peculiarly derivative out of the circumstances of Wonderland, whose citizens must increasingly sensitize their perceptions to the reality of impersonal sociological currents. A factor which has existed throughout historical times, the drive was much less clearly visible in the stable institutions of a relatively static community than in the twentieth century, where the increased tempo and magnified power illuminate the stark contours of this pervasive phenomenon. When institutions might endure for centuries amidst the slower pace of economic and political change, and when visible alterations were likely to be the abrupt, violent work of a particular group, its manifestations could readily be attributed purely to the lust for power of individuals. The peasant in Wonderland, who once bowed before the tangible symbols of royal majesty or trembled at the power-radiating cavalcade of armored horsemen, must now discern the fundamental social forces underlying all tangible political and social forms — like the scientist who has penetrated beyond the solid environment of the physical senses into the universe of energies.

That despotism which harassed the peasant in the old order, and whose restless, probing presence he still senses in Wonderland, emanates out of the cohesive currents of the social group. No longer required to obey the orders of a seigneur, he has passed directly under the lordship of the group itself, whose organizational energies generate a momentum potentially far more tyrannical than the personal actions of an evil baron.

II

Taine once described the state as "a vast engine in the human community like any given industrial machine in a factory" and asserted that "no indignation need be cherished beforehand against its mechanism, whatever this may be." [3] On the contrary, precisely this *should* be the target for anger. That mechanism is more than inanimate factory machinery, for through the compulsions exercised upon its human cogs, it becomes a living entity. Not in any given institutions, but in the appetite for power common to all social organizations lies the enemy of liberty — tyranny is latent in all social organizations.

Advocates of reform, whether aiming at substituting one political system for another or merely the acquisition of additional social benefits, must reckon with the potentially dangerous momentum in organizational energies. Without an awareness of its potent, sometimes lethal, role in the complexity of forces unleashed, their calculations necessarily lack realism. In point of fact, most revolutionary movements have fallen afoul of the institutional drive, given rise themselves to powerful organizations whose inner logic and direction of development eventually snuffed out the liberty in whose name they had started. Especially in time of revolution,

[3] Hippolyte A. Taine, *The Modern Regime,* Vol. I, pp. 110–111.

when other restraining organizations may have been smashed, is the opportunity open for the swift consummation of a new drive.

Popular history is frequently written in terms of a struggle between liberty and tyranny wherein characteristics of right-eousness and wickedness are attributed to these respective parties. Though considerable truth may sometimes reside in such elementary designations — and, of course, the presence of good and evil personalities in the narrative heightens emotional partisanship — the whole picture is not only much too simple, it often misses the point. Some of the so-called tyrants, far from being wicked men personally, were responsible statesmen of personal integrity, men doing their duty. Autocrats may be conscientious spokesmen for the institutional drive who labor in the honest conviction that centralized control will further the public welfare.

One might more realistically sweep aside the emotional connotations and see in this aspect of the historical phenomena a series of alternating movements to strengthen or weaken institutions. The end result of the evolution of an institution, or of an interlinked group of them, may be the imposition of controls beyond the needs or customs of the people; a tyrant is the visible human symbol for the deeper drive — the institutional dynamics run wild. Liberty may result from the destruction of a power monopoly, but the struggle for liberty may also be spearheaded by groups who are themselves potential with equally powerful drives. From this point of view, these drifts to absolutism and the struggles for freedom are the colorful tableaux of the invisible forces inherent in social organization as they materialize in the shapes and action of groups engaged, on the one hand, in defending hard-won areas of control and, on the other, in seeking full identity or self-expression.

Because a pattern wherein everyone's conduct is completely

regularized is of enormous convenience to those who must govern, this becomes the goal, consciously or not, on the state level or in major associations, of the institutional drive. Busy officials find it much the easier to measure by inflexible standard rules rather than employ the more just and benevolent personal judgments which all too often will subsequently weaken the regulatory hand in another instance. Broad regulations perforce are guided by the common denominators of the group or community and will override or frustrate spheres of more complex activity; broad rules are doomed to be nearly always wrong because the application must always be too general. Where the organization achieves fulfillment, it becomes an impersonal, soulless machine, automatically sorting and using people as though they were pawns, not human beings. Then the words of Leo Tolstoy, penned from his experiences under Tsarist power, provide an accurate portrayal of how the intense institutional drive looks to those who are regarded as mere objects to be governed:

> If a psychological problem were set to find means of making men of our time — Christian, humane, simple, kind people — perform the most horrible crimes without feeling guilty, only one solution could be devised: to go on doing what is being done. It is only necessary that these people should be governors, inspectors, policemen; that they should be fully convinced that there is a kind of business, called government service, which allows men to treat other men as things.[4]

In Tolstoy's writings one often encounters a sharp awareness of the anguish of the sacred human personality caught in the impersonal functioning of social organization, and certainly it was fitting symbolism that this "most Christian writer of modern times" should be excommunicated by his

---

[4] Leo N. Tolstoy, *Resurrection,* translated by Louise Maude (London, 1928), p. 362. [Vol. 19 of *The Works of Leo Tolstoy* (London, 1928–1937)]

Church because he dared to assert the primacy of true spiritual values over ecclesiastical (that is, largely institutional) aspects.

Men who are not prepared to submit to a conformity comfortable to the custodians of an institution always pose problems, and the more so because their superior abilities are otherwise recognizably needed by the organization. A reasonably mature, sophisticated institution tries to give them enough vested interest in the organization to see personal advantage in putting their talents at its service. Perhaps they can be persuaded to tolerate the broad doctrines exactly for what they are meant to be, a means for expressing truth as it exists for the masses, while they themselves, with circumspection, wander in a wider frame of reference; they must, however, at all times be sufficiently sensitive to institutional values not to jeopardize its security. This point is admirably illustrated by the famous trial of Galileo.

Church officials were exceedingly reluctant to move against him, and all they asked was that he disguise his belief in the heliocentric theory in terms not challenging dogma, a matter of tactics which, they felt, a reasonable man should be willing to concede. When Galileo failed to help them out of their painful dilemma by this concession, institutional compulsions forced them, unwillingly, to act. "Where responsibility began, perception ceased; and the top echelons, as we can see now, seem to have thought of intellectual issues purely as a matter of administration." [5] For the sake of institutional welfare, basic values had to be superseded by administrative.

For the insecure organization, successes must be institutional successes, but scapegoats must shoulder the blame when affairs go awry, since the machine itself cannot be acknowledged to be in error. The purges conducted by the Russian Communist party under Stalin are a dramatic example of

[5] Giorgio de Santillana, *The Crime of Galileo* (Chicago, 1955), p. 92.

how this procedure can become a formal ritual, a part of the technique of government. Perhaps the more sophisticated victims, good party members and quite aware of the socio-logical significance of the deed from their long associations with the party, would eventually go through the act with a certain sense of self-sacrifice, of giving their all for the good of the party. They might feel themselves blood sacrifices for the ultimate good, for the earth god who resides in blaring trumpets, beating drums, and red banners.

From the point of view of economic and social reality, the performance was absurd, but the sociological forces of the institution exerted their unrestrained coercion over everyone, including the leaders. No wonder that, after the death of Stalin, even the men holding the top positions sought to escape from the more extreme manifestations of the drive. Or that from within the Communist movement could come persons like Milovan Djilas to point directly at the culprit, the power appetite of the institution, which had so completely distorted the presumed shapes of their Communist community.

Countless examples from history could be cited of the juggernaut of the institutional drive smashing the finer crea-tions of human genius beneath its own clumsily massive advance. Although the drive, by creating social unity, makes a community possible, its grossest operations may hinder or prevent the full bloom of a civilization. Inevitably that Church which conserved within itself the highest values and deepest insights of the Western tradition and was able to do so only because of a superior institutional development, would, in its long history, pose the perpetual dilemma of all organiza-tions, the constant tensions between individuals who emphasize individualized human values (or divine values in the human being) and those whose positions entail responsibility for the whole structure. Even an organization as spiritual as the Fran-ciscans, originating in the saintly and unworldly activities of

St. Francis, nevertheless soon developed an institutional psychology, with concomitant tensions between representatives of the two outlooks.

When the institutional-minded attitude of administration gained excessive predominance in any decision, there might be a heavy price to pay, as in the indulgence controversy that triggered the Protestant Reformation. By treating Luther's original complaint of misuse of indulgences as the work of a troublemaker (i.e., one who makes trouble for the administrators) rather than as a popular and valid protest against the flouting of the Church's own laws, those responsible opened the way for a far greater challenge to their authority. The elements of Catholicism which the Protestants then assailed were, above all, those which had evolved out of administrative experience over the centuries, and without which the Church could scarcely have survived. The Protestants themselves, however, found their own churches, in most instances, immediately captured by another institutional drive, that of the Crown, and in their inability to maintain their autonomy in the sixteenth century may be discerned the necessities which had stimulated the growth of such elements in the medieval church. Later, of course, Protestant sectarians, in their own drive for liberty from the state church, developed the prototype of the modern association, thereby initiating a whole new approach to the problem.

Probably the single most savage attack on the mother Church of Western Europe came out of Russia, that land where the threat of governmental power always weighed so heavily on the human soul: Dostoevski's story of the Grand Inquisitor, where an institution turns upon its Founder and rejects His ideas. Implicit here is the charge that the values of the established organization had completely superseded the insights by which it originally was called into existence. This story reminds one of the Founder's own climactic hour when, in another confrontation between the institutional drive and the individual, Caiaphas explained: "It is expedient that one man shall die for the people, and the nation perish not." There spoke the voice of the institution. The key word was "expedient," a word utterly damning from one point of view, and yet, from the other side, summing up the tragic compulsions upon those who must manipulate power.

Into Lord Acton's famous aphorism, that power tends to corrupt and absolute power corrupts absolutely, could be read a different meaning than a moral deterioration of character; perhaps, in many instances, a man's conduct reflects the degree of compulsion upon him from the institutional drive. Under its dictation, he is not so much immoral as amoral; he is responding to the set of impersonal circumstances within which he works and whose effects upon those under him may seem evil. In Tsarist Russia an idea was afloat that the people should not be asked to exercise political authority because it would inevitably corrupt them. Enough that one man, the Tsar, should take upon himself the burden of sacrificing his soul, or of wrestling constantly with his conscience, in the interests of the people. However much one may recognize the rationalization for despotism, one can also perceive an awareness of the amoral atmosphere in which the administrator functions as he obeys the requirements of the institution. On the level of the despotic state, especially, where bloody tools are used and governmental processes grind on with little concern for the suffering or death of an individual, the abyss between private ethics and the actions of state officials might induce such an attitude.

Like that of the physician, the work of the administrator combines prestige with the frequent soul-racking situations in which the fate and lives of men are involved. Both must learn to ease the impact of onerous decisions on their consciences by making themselves the human instruments for rules and formulas, the wisdom of their crafts. Before the advent of Wonderland, the rationale of those responsible for the security of the institution was always based on the fear that the loosening of the cement that holds society together would topple the entire structure. In Pareto's world, this was often true; any sign of weakness brought rebellion. A challenge to authority must therefore set the machinery into punitive action lest "the nation perish." Always over a Caiaphas, however, hung the cynical suspicion, justified or not, that it was not the fate of the nation that concerned him as much as that *his own* leadership perish not.

In Wonderland, emancipation comes to the leader as well as to his followers. In the security of his organization, he is freed from the diabolic compulsions, from the more extreme measures of his craft. Modern politics, like medicine, has produced its own forms of anaesthesia. In Wonderland is encouraged that institutional drive which is imbedded in the very nature of social and political growth, which gives a healthy tone to society, and without which society disintegrates. In this community, however, men are also freed from the necessities of enslavement under its excesses and abuses. A leader who stands at the focus of institutional compulsions less tyrannical than formerly also encounters, increasingly, the multiple pressures exerted by the autonomy of the individual personality. Genuine liberty prevails only to the extent that the traditional code of ethics, matured primarily on the level of individual relationships, is brought to bear upon the custodians of the drive, who, in turn, are in a position to temper their own obedience to institutional exigencies.

III

For the immigrant to Wonderland, the freedom of the citizen is at least as much bound up with the future development of the associations as with the institutional drives of government. However much liberty may be jeopardized by the long-term encroachment of creeping statism (or by the immediate imposition of strong controls, if a garrison state becomes necessary), a reasonably untrammeled evolution of society must increasingly bring to public attention the role of the institutional drive in the associations. That political age would seem to be drawing to a close, in some of the nations in Wonderland, when crusades for the underprivileged could evoke mass support; once the community has achieved the productivity and the distribution system required to fulfill the material wants of its population, the political frame of reference must necessarily reflect the change. The emphasis will then increasingly shift to other fields of public concern, one of which should be the power drives, the excessive claims of organized bodies in the community.

Whatever the ideal may be, in practice the major associations now tend to concentrate their strongest efforts on attempts to use the state machinery for their own purposes. Aside from military necessities, the demands by organized groups for governmental intervention on their behalf must surely be the greatest factor in facilitating the institutional drive of the twentieth-century state. A part of the democratic processes since inception, their proportionate role in governmental policies has steadily increased, paralleling their growing strength in other ways; public opinion reacts by becoming increasingly critical of associational behavior, either in the excessive influence on state institutions or in the disregard for the welfare of others.

In the superlative ability to express the active forces of the present community, not in any claims to perfection, lies a principal justification for the associational system. Out of this very virtue springs perhaps its greatest remaining flaws; although providing more than adequate representation for men in strong associations, the effect upon those not protected in this way can be utterly disastrous. They are, quoting David Riesman, "in devastating competition with the not yet grouped" and "The only followers left in the United States today are those unorganized and sometimes disorganized unfortunates who have not yet invented their group." [6] Over a period of time, associational pressures, rather than inherent value to the community, tend to determine the income and status of a group. Organization pays dividends as those most skillful in the practices of an associational age become the privileged.

"In one respect," says Key, "the chief problem of the sovereign state is to prevent private associations from injuring the general public." [7] As organization consolidates, associations become highly effective veto groups. Too many sacred cows then graze in the verdant pastures of the vested associational interests. National leadership increasingly falls to those adept at playing, in Riesman's phrase, the "croquet game of the veto groups." [8]

Inasmuch as the associational commonwealth, barring catastrophe, is most unlikely to be abolished, the only alternative is for the unorganized to "invent" their own effective organization. Only by recognizing the facts of life in the modern community and acting upon them can the hitherto ungrouped hope to achieve some balancing of the scales of justice. Though in some instances a proper organization

[6] David Riesman, with Nathan Glazer and Reuel Denny, *The Lonely Crowd: A Study of the Changing American Character,* abridged (New York, 1955), p. 247.
[7] V. O. Key, Jr., *Politics, Parties, and Pressure Groups,* 2nd ed., p. 149.
[8] David Riesman, *The Lonely Crowd,* p. 246.

may not be physically feasible, while still others may lack the means, by themselves, to make their collective voice heard, rather large areas of the population (as, for instance, the American public in the role of consumers) suffer the ill effects of the associational system because they are themselves not actively participating in it.

Inherent in the system are two characteristics of leadership whose influences on the political scene are always irritating and occasionally dangerous. The governing group is prone to be more extreme than the followers, hence unduly accentuating whatever cause is being represented. Partly derived from the imperatives of the leadership position, this also results from the tendency of the more devoted persons to gravitate into the policy-making circle, from whence their intransigent and dogmatic views are expressed in the name of the whole group as though these opinions actually were representative of them all. The other characteristic is related to it, a frequent narrowness of outlook, due to the concentration of experience within the bounds of the one group only. The more obstinately the leaders of the various associations cling to their clan views, the more frustrated is that art of compromise which is the very essence of Wonderland's government.

In coping with these innate defects, the concept of the institutional drive can become an immensely valuable tool for public opinion as a standard implicit in the operation of the associational equilibrium; that is, within the context of Wonderland an institutional drive of an exaggerated degree has become immoral, because, in the security of the community, it is no longer necessary. Even more clearly does this standard apply to another class of weaknesses, obvious abuses by those organizations which eagerly make use of the liberties and opportunities of the associational system without imposing upon themselves the restraints commonly accepted in any democratic community.

A veneer of democracy, corresponding to the prevalent mode in its environment, covers even the most autocratically operated associations in the United States. No dispute is likely to be aroused, however, by the assertion that in some areas the practice of genuine self-government or adherence to the spirit of the Bill of Rights has not approximated that in the political sphere of the state. To a certain extent, the failure to maintain a directorate responsible to the membership derives out of the nature of the original smaller group; that is, practices perfectly legitimate within a group bound by personal relationships and expressing itself through a consensus of opinion may linger on even though sheer size has outmoded their feasibility. Quite obviously, too, if an organization is to be effective, a much stronger control over the members may be required in some occupational associations, such as the larger labor union, than in, for instance, societies of professional people. Anything less than strong authority is, unfortunately, no authority at all, for some individuals. Even in a country long experienced in political democracy, rather large groups of persons remain whose political capacities are still on the level which characterized the bulk of the populace before Wonderland, and their group directorates are likely to assume traits kindred to autocratic political regimes. In Europe, let it be recalled, this type of strong leadership is often provided by the Communists.

In some instances, however, practices have obtained which are in flagrant contradiction to those long since established on the political level of the state. Lack of regular elections in some labor union, to take one well-known example, permitted the perpetuation of the same group of leaders year after year. Where elections were held by a show of hands rather than by the secret ballot, the results possessed no more genuine validity than in a totalitarian plebiscite, nor do those where the local election of delegates is controlled by a national machine. Regardless of the provisions in their original charters, leaders have been known to rule by decree and enforce their edicts by methods more resembling a dictatorial state than the democratic community of which they are a part. Equally important, even as the community must permit the associations to develop freely in order to have adequate expression of all views and drives, so the association, in turn, should not allow its own drive to throttle the diverse voices in its own subdivisions. Relative internal freedom permits the flexibility of a continuing evolution, of changing emphases and policies as circumstances alter.

Associations require freedom to organize, the liberty to express their program before the public, the right to attempt the implementation of their policies. At the same time that the association is entitled to the maximum possible autonomy, it cannot violate those conditions which make its own existence possible. (Members who regard any outside attempt at restraining their actions as an attack upon the organization itself would do better to put their loyalties to work within the group in such a way that such intervention becomes unnecessary.) Even as democratic practices virtually originated in the training school of certain associations, so malpractices in the associations can in time corrode the machinery of political government also. Correcting abuses of associational liberty, restraining those groups whose practices are not in accord with Wonderland, is a function of the self-regulatory balance of power, which eventually turns against the guilty group. Through the American democratic processes, an aroused public has, on occasion, been able to restrain the conduct of business corporations as well as, through antitrust legislation, to retard the trend toward monopoly, and the same type of reaction now sometimes manifests itself against irresponsible or excessively ambitious associations. Particularly needed, however, for the sake of a quicker and more effective enforcement, is a greater public awareness of the possibilities existing in the equilibrium for encouraging associational restraint, wherever necessary.

Beyond these weaknesses and abuses lies a more basic phenomenon, the danger that lurks in the long-term effects of the institutional drive on the hitherto democratic association. In the course of stabilizing an organization, a core of leaders entrenches its position and installs specialized groups trained purely for administration. To some extent, this is a necessary step, one which provides skilled leadership and necessary continuity; indeed, long-enduring associations like the traditional churches create cadres as a matter of course. Yet, as Edward Hallett Carr points out in *The New Society,* it is very likely to lead progressively to an undue division of labor between the leaders and the remainder of the group.[9] This represents a decisive move away from democracy, beyond the government of a local association by the "elders," and it constitutes a change in principle, a crossing of the divide between democratic practices and authoritarianism.

Upon this emerging core, which directs the dynamic policies of expansion, control, and discipline, public attention should be centered, as the group leaders inevitably seek to follow the natural tendency of all institutions. As Reinhold Niebuhr puts it in *Moral Man and Immoral Society,* "Power, once attained, places the individual or the group in a position of perilous eminence so that security is possible only by the extension of power." [10] Its principal interests will shift from fulfilling the original functions of the association to the means

---

[9] Edward Hallett Carr, *The New Society* (London, 1951), pp. 77–78.
[10] Reinhold Niebuhr, *Moral Man and Immoral Society: A Study in Ethics and Politics* (New York, 1936), p. 42.

of maintaining power; values overweighted by pragmatic experiences of an institutional sort increasingly replace the intrinsic. Methods will be stressed for enhancing the authority of the leaders over the rank and file, and "the organization man" molded to fit the smoothly functioning machine.

In the continuing trends to consolidation, the historian will see the pattern of evolution in earlier organizations beginning to assert itself, a process which, if continued, would culminate in an oligarchic, bureaucratic institution. The channels between leaders and followers would gradually be closed, and, eventually, neither influence nor ambitious men rise out of the ranks to leaven the administrative psychology. Associational conduct formalizes into traditional modes of behavior, the inflexibility and internal overspecialization rendering more and more difficult any adjustment to new circumstances as they appear. Righteously indignant at upstarts, it then defends itself against opponents with typically heavy-handed blows and cumbersome movements. In a static society it may survive indefinitely — in a changing world its own institutional drive has doomed it to disaster at the hands of new and vital groups or through the secession of its own dissatisfied elements.

Of a piece with this whole development is the continuing expansion of the major organizations. If these groups are permitted to grow according to their own nature, they may eventually congeal into permanent power structures, each one tending to mature its embryonic state form into a more complete institution. Although they might still, for a time, balance one another and prevent any single one from gaining control of the state by itself, the lesser groups nevertheless would lose autonomy, and with them the great variety of opinions, and voices, and needs of a modern society be muffled, and submerged. Carried to the ultimate conclusion, this evolution would also bring political control over a nation divided into a score of powerful organizations, which in turn would manipulate the state machinery in accordance with their own needs.

One may look back, with foreboding eye, upon the course of events in many city states where coalitions of guilds entrenched themselves for long periods of time, while within each guild arose a closed circle of leaders who kept the power for themselves generation after generation. If the pattern of earlier organizational evolution were an infallible guide to the future, one could have little doubt of what will happen, for then the institutional drive would continue to impel the creation of gigantic organizations which eventually will affiliate with or merge into the state. To be sure, the climactic moment might occur when a Caesar, speaking for the people against these vested interests, would forcibly impose the will of *all* the people upon the self-centered groups. Long before this point was reached, however, the association would have abandoned its own nature and proper function, henceforth being fit only to serve as an administrative agency of the state.

The most ominous sign of all is the obvious fact that the expansion of the major associations reflects the general trend in the twentieth-century community. To quote Carr again: "And with the mammoth trust and the mammoth trade union came the mammoth organ of opinion, the mammoth political party and, floating above them all, the mammoth state, narrowing still further the field of responsibility and action left to the individual and setting the stage for a new mass society." [11]

Not in this generation will the question be settled whether the present organizational setup in Wonderland is only a transitory phase on the way to a community dominated by a few giant state-affiliated associations of an institutional character. In part, the reassertion of the old cycle depends upon the probability of a reversion to a static society; at present,

[11] Edward H. Carr, *The New Society*, p. 64.

under the continued impulse of technological innovations, the community seems far more likely to face a prolonged era of incessant social adjustment similar to that underway for the past century or more. Though individual associations may, within limits imposed by their environment, assume the internal characteristics of an overly successful institutional drive, this same environment, remaining creative and plastic, would bring forth new organizations which, to the extent that they represent the new forces better, would supplant the older ones in positions of chief influence.

Another possibility, to be discussed later, is a fundamental change in the character of the national state; by imposing a somewhat different set of circumstances, this would simultaneously alter the course of associational development.

Quite possibly, also, the growth of Wonderland has brought into being elements which make possible the permanent emancipation from the excesses of the drive. Universal education, the pervasiveness of ideas through swift communications, the deeply rooted sense of individuality, the habitual mentoring by historical experience, the deepening perception of sociological forces, the apparently growing ability to control community evolution by political action — these are some of them. Perhaps mankind is thus forging the tools which will make it the master, not the prisoner, of the forces inherent in social organization.

IV

Of all institutional drives, that of the state is the most powerful, the most dangerous, and the most difficult to restrain. Wonderland's greatest political achievement to date has consisted in a dispersal of power sufficient to tame the state's will to the wishes of its citizens. It remains strong government, nevertheless, having at its disposal the customary physical weapons of state, and which, by reason of the dogmas, taboos, and habits of obedience clustering about it, can resort, with the most public acquiescence, to extraordinary measures.

Though threats to its security is the greatest stimulant for its drive, just as in the associations, the state persistently widens and strengthens its power for other reasons also. In democratic countries the peacetime institutional drive is expressed partially through bureaucratic proliferation but achieves its major breakthroughs by being *called forth* by organized elements in the population. Endowed with ample powers and weapons for coping with particular or general emergencies, the state grows primarily through improvised functions, assumed in periods of crisis, becoming permanent. The citizen of Wonderland, cognizant of past history and only too well aware of how the state has devoured many a community in this century, must needs be alarmed lest the cumulative effect generate a momentum enabling its own drive to escape the restraints of the equilibrium.

Despite the profound changes of the past two hundred years, the course of political events in the era immediately prior to the advent of Wonderland in Western Europe still conveys a sombre warning to the present generation. In the earlier phases of the evolution to royal despotism between the fifteenth and eighteenth centuries, the increasing strength of the Crown obviously was a necessary ingredient for the growth of the European countries and the well-being of their peoples. For the king and his ministers, the logic of each extension of power may have seemed irresistible, inasmuch as the reduction of vested interests was, beyond a doubt, immediately conducive to the general welfare. Once royal sources of revenue, military strength, and central position overbalanced the other organizations and institutions, and national parliaments proved ineffective as a source of government or as a restraint on the Crown, the momentum of central authority carried it into despotism.

Analyzed in detail, however, the military circumstances of the national monarchies of the era would be found to be a major, perhaps the determining, factor in the developing despotism. Wherever political units are in competition with one another, the usual effect of insecurity upon the institutional drive occurs: an intensity of drive in rough ratio to the necessities of successful rivalry in their environment. In a situation fraught with extreme peril, the organization, if possessed of resources and able leadership, will mobilize the more thoroughly and resort to methods the more boldly desperate. Neither mathematically measurable nor occurring with the certainty of laws of physical energies, this reaction nevertheless manifests itself with enough probability to make it an immensely important factor in the basic interactions among rival entities, despite the obtuseness of leadership, vagaries of group behavior, and the resistant inertia of organizational habits.

Numerous instances could be cited where threatened states have adjusted by increasing centralization and militarization. Modern Prussia immediately comes to mind as a country strongly molded in the crucible of military rivalries and by its discipline attaining a weight nearly equal to its larger competitors. As for a unified Germany later, Prince Bülow expressed the situation thus: "The German Empire situated in the middle of Europe and insufficiently protected by Nature on the frontiers, is and must remain a military State; and strong military States have always required monarchical guidance." [12] If in a nonmonarchical age one construes the last two words to mean the continuity of strong central government, the statement exactly describes the situation leading to a strong drive. Other examples could be given,

[12] Quoted by George P. Gooch, *Germany,* pp. 105–106.

such as the characteristic development of strong military units on the frontiers of Germany, or the Caliphate, or China, wherever endemic warfare placed a premium upon it.

By contrast, a Great Britain protected by the English Channel never did require a large peacetime military establishment in its period of greatness, and the British, not needing the strong guidance of autocracy, were enabled to experiment with a parliamentary regime. The Americans long enjoyed the luxury of protection by the oceans, and the more recent strengthening of the federal government reflects, to a considerable extent, the onset of the prevalent conditions of insecurity. A prolonged period of tension, like that of the Cold War, could indeed mold the political communities in the direction of an approximation of those in George Orwell's *1984*.

Fascism, a twentieth-century phenomenon whose diverse aspects defy the convenience of any single definition, derives its external habiliments and much of its dogma out of the extreme rivalries among nations, and its end result is a state grossly overorganized for purposes of international conflict. It is also a malady springing directly out of the breakdown of the normal community when economic malaise or political weaknesses reduce the effectiveness of the associational equilibrium. One or more organizations, representing frustrated or desperate segments of the population, reject the methods of Wonderland in favor of purely pragmatic techniques for winning total power. Gaining widespread popular support by reason of the prevailing crisis, and its triumph greatly facilitated through the inability of the normal groups to react with unified opposition, such an organization may seize power. The exacerbated nationalism caused by the people's sense of insecurity in turn provides the means for imposing the utmost centralization and complete discipline upon the community.

That is, fascism results, in essence, from the convergence of two generically identical sets of forces which have been operating on two separate levels, within the national community and on the international level; conditions of insecurity evoke such an intense institutional drive on each level that the natural forces of the equilibrium are overwhelmed and the normal structure of Wonderland shattered. One abnormal, politically oriented, association coalesces with the community nucleus, the state, causing the latter to flare into enormously magnified power; any organized expressions of the forces of gravitation and repulsion in the equilibrium are forcibly extinguished, and all of the elements in the community are drawn into one compact mass, the totalitarian state.

Far from being a specific historical episode limited to such countries as Germany and Italy, fascism remains a potential political malady in any advanced country. It seems particularly apt to occur in a nation far along the transition to Wonderland where the equilibrium has, however, not yet matured into a stable balance of power. In a severe, long-term conflict among groups during a major crisis, the one which accepts most completely the implications of warlike conditions, and which consequently steps outside the bounds of lawful, democratic group conduct, enhances its likelihood of victory over its stunned or hypnotized adversaries. Just as the most militarized state will win wars, all other things being equal, so the most centralized, disciplined, and ruthless social group will most probably triumph on the domestic scene under conditions of desperate rivalry and consequent insecurity. In its present-day accumulation of channelized power, the state is an object of irresistible temptation for abnormally ambitious groups, an instrument ready-made which confers almost supernatural domination over the lives of the populace, once the group has penetrated into the sacred precincts from whence emanate laws. If this structure can be seized by the organization, the means are then available, just as in the case of the Communists, for attempting the reproduction in the animate and inanimate surroundings of those particular visions which obsess the group.

In the course of the struggle, the victorious organization discarded the normal community values in favor of a special set of values based purely upon institutional survival itself. Tools useful in the struggle both as regards grappling with other groups and controlling their own members, are then applied, when triumphant, to the entire population. The most completely knit group thus imprints its ethos upon a country, with long-enduring consequences in the purely institutional values which become the basic law of the land.

Written on the pages of the world's history — sometimes as a marginal account and sometimes as the main theme — is the record of warfare between civilized metropolises and barbarian tribes. Civilizations have repeatedly been overthrown by these assaults from without. That which occurs in Wonderland or in the transition to it, as a result of the struggle among social groups, is the upsurgence of attitudes and practices in the sharpest contrast to the direction of political development in civilized countries. A new form of barbarism, which might be termed *institutional barbarism,* has emerged where the institutions themselves are responsible for individual acts of such a nature, and which is born, not out of cultural backwardness in the customary sense, but out of the competition among organizations.

To the peril of this unexpected denouement has the evolution of modern society, its technological revolution and accelerated tempo of the institutional drive, brought the modern community. If the equilibrium of channelized social energies begins to break down, the tensions generated will breed overorganization and the lack of political direction be remedied by the imposition of a social order held together by exaggerated institutional values. Fascist and Communist dictators then employ devices of political power based upon the usage of institutional barbarism. An age which has devised new tools for begetting and controlling the energies of the physical universe also produces tools and techniques for organizing social energies, the very inventions in communications and transportation which were so potent in the evolution of Wonderland also making possible the total incorporation of all areas into the governmental edifice. Without them, Mussolini's ideal of "Everything in the state, nothing outside of the state, nothing against the state" would have been impossible. The ultimate culmination of the institutional drive, its *reductio ad absurdum,* is to be seen in these forms spawned amidst the rivalries of an emerging Wonderland.

In the complete fulfillment of the institutional drive lies a despotism which returns man to barbarism. Although he is learning to tame the forces of the physical universe to his control, he may also become the prisoner of the forces in society. Necessarily subject to the basic currents and intrinsic patterns of society born out of human beings associating together, the citizen of Wonderland must never forget the dark shapes which the inner logic of organizational exigencies and the unrestrained institutional drive can bring into physical reality. Resistance to despotism does not begin with a Hitler or Stalin, but earlier, in a deep suspicion of all aggrandizement of power. In a clear perception of this drive and its consequences we see a means to gradual emancipation from this hitherto inevitable bondage, for social ties are shown to be practical, pragmatic tools whose justifications are limited to the realistic and functional, and whose limitations are dictated by considerations of the inviolability of the human personality. It strips away pretense and dogma and reveals the group, and its action, for what it is, when it passes beyond legitimate practices.

In our century where rapid change, surging power, and incubating multiplicity combine to focus attention upon the social processes rather than upon social forms, the concept of the institutional drive could serve as a unifying principle. The developments of the transition to Wonderland force upon the public mind a keen awareness of certain fragmentary and one-sided aspects of it, such as "creeping socialism" and the class struggle. These have been battle cries, partisan expressions for a portion of the whole process. It is time that they all be merged by the usage of a more universal concept which probes to the very heart of the matter, to the basic laws of social cohesion.

The concept is a two-edged sword; it cuts deeply into the tissues of contemporary institutions. While we may relish its destruction of shibboleths in some directions, in others it may challenge our own most cherished loyalties. We are all, to some extent, psychologically mobilized under the standards of one or more of these. The institutional drive, when its role is objectively delineated, becomes the ultimate atheism of *earthly* gods and hence infinitely more heretical, for the fanatic mind, than the denunciation of one such tribal god in order to preach another. At the very least, the concept furnishes a sociological base for the rejuvenation of a liberalism of a kind that preaches liberation not only from the state but from other overly possessive ties.

When the peasant entered the gates of the American Wonderland he looked upon the Statue of Liberty as the symbol of a new freedom. As other, more backward peoples approached Wonderland, they, too, set up statues of liberty in the form of constitutional charters and assemblies which proclaimed the era of freedom. As events turned out all too often, freedom was less than complete, for tyranny was not permanently overthrown by the end of a tsar or kaiser or of a fascist or Communist regime. The institutional drive, like electricity, powers modern society, but tyranny is as close to all of us as death from the careless grasping of a high voltage electric wire.

7

THE POLITICAL INFERNO

The terrorism of institutional barbarism is not enough, in itself, to assure continued mastery over a nation by a dictatorial regime. Accompanying it must be a sweeping and dynamic structure of political faith powerful enough to marshal the people into unified action. Though the dogmas and symbols of fascism and Communism may be quite different, the basic configurations into which their respective mythologies are cast are fundamentally similar, and so is the framework of any intensely nationalistic type of faith, because they are all primarily based on that essentially modern phenomenon, the collective political mind of a whole people as it asserts itself in the lowest possible common denominator.

Political leaders in Wonderland, in fact, must also be constantly aware of two kinds of reality, the actual shapes and forces of their society and the more simplified version of it possessed by most citizens. Although the contrast between the two is most starkly evident in the authoritarian state, where propaganda can paint a picture wildly inconsistent with true conditions, the difference is to a lesser degree also apparent in democracies. Not only the peasant immigrant to Wonderland, but also the long established habitant, requires a simplified approach to politics.

An individual, absorbed in his many nonpolitical interests, cannot be a full time citizen. Where he is directly involved, for example where his economic affairs are concerned, no observer of democracy in action would question his capacity for intelligent participation, but few minds are trained or sufficiently experienced to perceive or utilize the mental shorthand of ideas and insights necessary for an adequate comprehension of the total social, economic, and political reality. Just as a man need not be a mechanical engineer when driving an automobile, so he need not be a political scientist in order to be a citizen. In practice, the voter, even at his best, does not so much express a sound judgment in statecraft as he reflects the social forces bearing upon him; that is, in voicing his needs and problems he contributes his mite of political energy to those broad forces which weave the patterns of contemporary history.

Without indulging in too great a caricature, one can sketch the basic configurations within which the political thought of the great majority in all countries tends to be expressed. In sum, this collective political mind constitutes an influential factor in the evolving world of Wonderland, and one which, as it imagines a society at variance with the actual physical reality, inevitably tends to distort the logical course of development. Upon it is built the politics of a nation, insofar as its popular expression is concerned. In terms of the total doctrinal edifice, it could be likened to the girders of a building, upon which may be imposed various styles of architecture. What, then, are the elementary concepts or ways of thinking, the common denominator level, whereby the average citizen visualizes the political life of the nation?

Almost inevitably, the natural focus of attention will continue to be the governmental personalities of the time; since these men are invested with the symbols of power, the course of events is directly attributed to the way in which they wield that power. The pressures which play upon statesmen, the more remote but compelling currents formed by the interplay of these forces over a period of time, the logic of institutional welfare, the ineluctable framework of immediate circumstances, only fragments of these will be visible to the unaided eye of the citizen. The ancient peasant, living with forces of nature he could not understand, provided himself with explanations within his reach by populating the physical world with human figures endowed with divine powers. Similarly, in our day the political figures walk the public stage and play their roles, symbolizing in themselves the drama being played out by forces oftentimes incomprehensible to the average citizen.

Living in a tangible environment, he expects clear-cut results to be achieved by decisions made and action taken: solid forms can be manipulated in a simple and direct setting things aright again. Believing in the efficacy of immediate action, he would solve problems by strong physical movement, the mobilization of the many in a crusade, the forward march, even the *ça ira* of revolution.

Action necessarily involves a struggle, a conflict between good and evil wherein the individual political figure is either a hero or a villain. The issues are moral and are as obvious as the difference between black and white; that is, even minor disputes, otherwise susceptible to rational, objective solutions, are likely to be visualized in terms of a skirmish in the current Armageddon of world philosophies. In its extreme form, this psychology is peculiarly attracted to explanations of events based upon the plot theory, that the evil can be explained by the work of villainous conspirators against the good people, while the same type of mentality may also lead individuals to participate in such schemes, to be naive enough to believe that conspiracies can actually better conditions or achieve good results.

Such is the inadequacy of human intelligence in dealing with the intricacies of modern society that the caricature inevitably must carry the burden of meaning for even the relatively keen thinker. For the wavering of the thought processes in one who is not at home in the world of ideas, psychological compensation is sought by the rigid clutching of one or several insights without ranging outward to the additional associations that accompany them. An untrained mind craves absolute truth possessing the reliability of the physically tangible. Ideas, hence, must have the stability and assurance, the texture, of dogma. Not only that, they must carry meanings in terms of action, and so, in simple fashion, these ideas convey a certain sense of relationships by the false means of becoming charged with an emotional quality. In politics, many persons are prone to seize upon one great insight and use it as a permanent standard for the solution of all problems; possessed by it, and deeply possessive of it, the citizen may remain fanatically uncomprehending of other possible insights and hence lack tolerance for their possessors.

Far more tangible and attractive than ideas is the membership in a group, which will provide a set of ready-made concepts within dimensions that can be reached. Those persons who require the presence of the herd, and who crave activity as its own virtue, are absorbed into the gang, and their judgments are determined by it. Loyalty becomes, in itself, more important than truth, or, more accurately, loyalty *is* truth.

One more aspect must surely be mentioned as characteristic, a parochialism in the time sense, the lack of that perspective which can be secured only from a greater awareness of the historical dimension than a set of traditions and homilies. Not possessing society's reservoir of memory in the sense of having learned the lessons of experience or the caution induced by past errors, they would commit the same mistake over and over again. More particularly, the processes of evolution, of continuity and change, are beyond the range of observation, and with them so much of the scope and direction of Wonderland.

This, in sketchy form, is the common denominator structure of political thought, upon which are mounted the more specific details of popular political philosophies. Whatever the natural forms and forces of contemporary historical processes, men translate them, by greater or lesser oversimplifications, into these elementary concepts and in so doing, in turn, often impose, through political action, artificial restraints or shapes. Every successful politician develops a sensitivity to the particular ways in which the structure manifests itself in his constituency. The predominance of this level of political thinking will often, perhaps usually, force the politician to cast his own political expressions into what he himself knows to be demagogy. In more politically backward countries, its influences may go farther and serve as a selective force driving the leaders to resort to demagogic slogans because only through their usage can power be exercised. Hence, Wonderland must be built with a clear comprehension of, and provision for, the seemingly inadequate capacity of the human mind to grasp fully the processes of which the citizen is a part.

A few generations ago it was generally believed that the average man could not govern himself, and this presupposition continues to underlie the actions of dictatorial leaders in our age. They assume that the people must be led by a vanguard of men who do know politics and that the act of government consists in the pragmatic manipulation of the populace according to the leaders' own notions of the welfare of society. True enough, the normal ways of thinking about politics by the average citizen, when compared to complex reality, are rudimentary; when they actually materialize into public life in a form approximating that in which they occur originally in the mind, a more elementary form of government inevitably results. Nevertheless, democratic governments have proven successful. Why do they survive instead of disintegrating, as pre-democratic writers insisted that they would? Why doesn't the mob appear more often, why don't the "masses," once so feared by conservative writers, destroy the democratic framework?

The answer lies in the regulatory machinery of democratic government that has grown up, through the gradual process of historical evolution, out of the interplay of social forces. As the public successfully enlarged its areas of control, instruments for the expression of its will came into existence which reflected the variety of motivations and ideas, while also transmuting them into forms suitable for the politics of the realm. In each step along the way a preceding development had created a felt maladjustment or problem, and out of a period of trial and error emerged a successful innovation, though often initially disguised in the trappings of older government. Throughout the crucial emergence of these political tools and practices, the citizen usually continued to clothe the successive episodes in the forms typical of the common denominator concepts of the times, while concurrently, in those particular matters in which he was vitally

engrossed and energetically active, his political energies unwittingly contributed to the creation of the new instruments
and practices. Generated on the level where group action
or government impinged most vitally upon the individual's
interests, these forces were enabled to assume directions in
approximate accordance with their natures, and then to find
expression in more formal organizational agencies. Thus these
instrumentalities superimposed themselves upon and channelized the elementary reactions and concepts of the individual.

While Wonderland was gradually creating its scientific and
technological aspects, it also, through the incessant persuasion
of its community realities, was inducing inventions in the
social and political realms which were equally a work of
genius. These are as real, as much rooted in the wholeness
of Wonderland, can no more be ignored or abandoned, than
can the scientific and economic achievements. The resultant
machinery functions almost as a matter of custom, as an automatic entity of its own. Those energies of the citizen which
by themselves would go off in chaotic directions or which
would necessitate dictatorship are channelized into constructive political patterns. The guarantee of stable government,
and of freedom, lies less in the democratic fervor of the individual than in the functioning of the very nearly autonomous
machinery itself.

As this structure maintains contact with the mind of the
electorate, it necessarily operates on the elementary level of
the common denominators. On this plane, simple ideas suf-
fused with emotional content must be employed, symbols and
slogans introduced which enlist the active support of a maximum number of people. Public attention is focussed upon
individual personalities in whose common qualities the voters
recognize themselves, and in whose achievements they feel
themselves justified. Crucial problems and issues, the whole

vibrant complexity of a society, are transposed into the
figures of men who must handle the levers of power. Perhaps
the two-party system forms an ideal outlet for an electorate
thinking its politics within a good-evil dichotomy. A mythology is devised and propagandized which will generate moral
fervor on one side or the other, only to be discarded in the
committee rooms of the legislative bodies, where more practical attitudes assume control. In this fashion, long since
ingrained in habitual patterns, is bridged the gap between the
practical goals of the democratic ideal and the crude political
concepts of the electorate, and energies are aroused which
broadly serve to register the interests and intents of various
sections of the community.

On the legislative and executive levels of this structure,
democracy maintains a permanent training school of experience wherein more precise and intimate knowledge of politics
is acquired. Ambitious men emerge out of the crowd of
citizens, individuals who are representative of their fellows,
and who, through long experience in various offices, educate
themselves in the art of the professional politician and quickly
learn their lessons in institutional logic. Meantime, the bulk
of the electorate maintains its rather bifurcated role, the
common denominator concepts for the broad sweep of national politics and a more positive educated viewpoint when
its own interests are directly concerned. In this fashion the
wondrous contrivance of democratic government creates its
own division of labor and sharpens the minds of participants
for their specific functional roles.

This system also works remarkably well where an evolutionary process is underway. The electorate is gradually educated to the various aspects of a maladjustment over a period
of time as its painful persistence demands remedial attention.
A particular problem, occurring in concrete form, forces
specific and practical answers wherein the naive conceptions

of the electorate must be discarded — though the initial measures are likely to be palliatives, they inaugurate a series of steps in a trial and error process, sometimes extending over many years' time, and out of which emerge solutions more in consonance with reality. In an imperfect world where politics is the art of the possible, the republic legislates and, under the tutelage of hard reality, ultimately is constrained to act wisely.

A better solution is provided than could be reached by any one person, no matter how wise or how much in touch with reality, or even by any one council of experts. All elements of society can scarcely be properly seated at such a gathering, or, if they could, the spokesmen would soon become a distinct group in their own right, and thus cease to be representative of society as a whole. Only the community can legislate for itself, the seemingly cumbersome methods now in effect in actuality ensuring a relative plasticity to the mold of circumstances.

If even the wisest individuals cannot attain the necessary competency, how much less true proficiency must be possessed by any group reaching dictatorial powers through methods of violence, and which will be far more likely to flaunt the crude characteristics of the collective public mind. Basically, the features of the modern totalitarian state seem to be a reflection of this psychology, a projection upon the national scene of a rudimentary political outlook. The emphasis on personality leads to the *Führer* principle, that a great man can lead a nation to success because he is endowed with extraordinary wisdom. Invariably, the totalitarians mobilize the people by picturing a gigantic struggle between good and evil, for which all sacrifices can be demanded and wherein the enemy deserves to be annihilated. The other-directed crowd, without strong principles of its own, constitutes an open invitation for opportunists or fanatics to satisfy its cravings for decisive action, while a few simple ideas, given the quality of dogma, become the basis for a political philosophy permeated with pseudo-religious emotions. With the entire superstructure of instrumentalities whereby the citizen is enabled to govern his country sheared off, the dictator does indeed represent the people, a people divested of effective individuality in social role and at their most inarticulate level.

The paradox that the fulfillment of dreams of national independence and popular government has often been followed by the appearance of dictatorships is more apparent than real, for, as the momentum of progress continues to sweep over the earth, peoples are given political power before possessing the means to express it. Lacking the decades and perhaps generations of maturation wherein a pattern of governmental participation beyond the natural local area becomes habitual, the mass migrants into Wonderland may only be able to express their national will through forms originating directly out of the collective political mind. Each people, hence, must mature its own pattern of popular representation as rapidly as possible, lest the raw, common denominator mind, usurping complete control, thrusts them into a modern Inferno. The same waters which can inundate and devastate, when properly dammed and channelized, will irrigate the fields and make the garden of the peasant to flourish.

II

As hopes for a better future have increasingly seemed justified, in an age of growing materialism governments have been compelled to postulate a paganized heavenly city of the twentieth-century politicians. Pressures for further improvements in living conditions have continued to mount, caused less by the poverty in which most men have always been mired than by the realization that for the first time an escape is tantalizingly within reach. An appetite which in America is continually whetted by commercial advertising has become a universal driving force, congealing in some countries, like hot, searing molten metal, into the iron of revolutionary weapons. Nevertheless, while mankind has fixed its aspirations on the attainment of an earthly paradise, events have proven the potential reality, just as in the religious dichotomy of heaven and hell, of an Inferno. The more important, then, that the peasant immigrant see not only the vision of the one, but also discern the snare of the other on the route to the promised land.

Under normal circumstances, where a natural and rational evolution is underway, the enlightened mind will scarcely be preoccupied with the existence of either a Wonderland or an Inferno. Words like "Inferno" and "Antichrist," when used in our environment, sound naive and overdramatic; our thoughts recoil from them in embarrassment, as if they were ghosts out of the medieval. Nevertheless, many other ghosts have reappeared in our era, practices which the optimistic men of the golden century of progress hoped were being exorcised forever. If mankind must visualize the unfolding drama in terms of good and evil, then the rightful shapes of *both* Wonderland and Inferno, each built by human hands in an era of godlike powers, must be made readily visible to human eyes.

Unfortunately for the predisposition of the common denominator mind, this Inferno has no single proper name. Just as the focussing of attention on personalities in lieu of the social forces grossly oversimplifies the situation, the attributing of good and evil to specific persons, organizations, or peoples is very likely to be a deceptive caricature of the actual situation. When the nations of the world have continued to dance the minuet, and one decade's foe is the next decade's friend, the exaggerations in attributing diabolical characteristics to the momentary rival should be readily apparent.

Evil does not cohere exclusively to any single organization, or country, nor are any of these likely to be exclusively evil. Having appeared in organized form under conditions which have borne a variety of names, fascism and communism among them, it could also materialize, in the future, under other labels. The potentiality exists in all countries, no matter how civilized, and in periods of distress and crisis any political community, including our own, could react in this direction.

At the same time, the sense of evil is a relative matter. The existence of Wonderland enhances the perception of a physical Inferno — the increasing light makes one more sensible of a greater blackness. For those accustomed to a more rude daily life, the conditions which the citizen of Wonderland would regard as an Inferno may seem normal, even as this may be true for the least sophisticated in Wonderland itself. Simultaneously, the more advanced groups in an underdeveloped country may chronically suffer a distress invisible to other elements of the population.

For the citizen of Wonderland, the contours of evil manifest themselves most insistently from within the totalitarian state. Its peculiar characteristics are molded, above all, by two basically formative factors, an invincible institutional drive and the direct hegemony of the collective political mind. The greater the drive within a community, the more intense is the inculcation of an incandescent mythology, be it based upon nation, or class, or sect; from the point of view of the men in charge of the political machinery, an effective set of beliefs in the community greatly eases the problem of ensuring co-operation or obedience. In order to achieve a strongly disciplined cohesion, the people must be fanatically imbued with values, dogmas, and goals in a form adapted to their mental grasp.

Through the ages the peasant had worshipped forces of nature which he could not truly fathom or master, and he had permitted intermediaries to exercise their professed arts of suasion upon the dominant spirits about him. Now that men comprehend physical nature, the ancient gods have ceased to exact belief, but that which cannot be completely understood or controlled are the forces of society, and these now, at times, become objects of devotion. Out of these forces come wars that wipe out millions. To the state, the citizen now pays his tithe and more. The man who loses his job and can get no other has felt the effects of a power beyond his control; in the ultimate consequences upon him and his, the devastations caused by the unfathomable social energies in his environment can exceed that of drought and hurricane. He cannot penetrate very deeply into the mysteries of the social processes, but a mythology, couched in terms of his own natural concepts, provides him with credible explanations, even as did the old superstitions for the works of nature.

By their sheer magnitude the stupendous forces now concentrated in the state loom as the largest power in the environment. Amidst the more recondite phenomena of society, the state is tangible, it is obvious reality; the patriotic ceremonial carries complete emotional conviction. Therefore, as the multitudes once worshipped the sun, they may now bow down and worship this sun of society, from which seems to flow omnipotent power. A reverence formerly directed to the deities who nourished or spoiled the crops is then, perhaps, focussed upon the broad valleys of the nation and the crop of human beings who grow therein, the blood of the race and the soil upon which the race thrives. In the last analysis, such a myth is now likely to amount to a cult of self worship, an adulation of the group itself as a collective entity.

The ultimate choice of a specific cult will vary from place to place. Mussolini, for instance, claimed to be a heretic of both Vatican and Kremlin, but nevertheless believed that man must have a myth. When he decided to raise a god for the people to worship, this quondam socialist's mind gravitated to the single strongest magnetic idea of his environment, that of the nation, whereas had he lived in another place or time, this opportunist would undoubtedly have chosen a different deity.

Such men are experts at carving idols, not the graven images of old, but shaping them out of the forms and forces of society, and, as the pagan clergy once invoked nature by their incantations, modern sorcerers now seek to control the energies of society by their magical spells. Mankind in assuming the prerogatives of gods through its control of nature, inevitably also assumed the power to call up false gods and to construct for them a temple of Inferno. Repeatedly in the twentieth century, high priests of such earth gods and opportunistic adventurers have thus appeared to rouse the destructive energies within the depths of the human soul. Where the vacuum of faith in our century has permitted, such forces — anger, hate, fear, jealousy, revenge, vindictiveness — emerge to stir the people to action. While the high priest leads his followers willingly and blindly, the adventurer may sell his soul for the aid of these forces — only to find that, once aroused, they are beyond his control, and even he must also obey them.

When these men seize the power apparatus of the state, a mythology materializes into a world of living men. In a society filled with the familiar shapes of Wonderland occurs a weird distortion; the physical environment of the community alters little. One might almost believe that nothing had changed, but the atmosphere has been transformed, as though all society were participating in the ritual of a satanic Sabbat. Those not blinded by the myth can see, as if in an hallucination, the barbarian stalking through the halls of civilization smashing with his battle-ax mind the finest intellectual creations of the ages. Devils, dressed as saints and heroes, butcher the saints and heroes while crying that these are the devils. Creeds and dogmas are chanted, drums roll, the tribal dances are enacted, the witch doctors hold service before the monoliths. The voices of legitimate Wonderland fall silent; the living spirit passes out of the social body of the nation.

This political Inferno aroused in our age is not always immediately identifiable in its true qualities, nor is it separated from Wonderland as though it were on another planet or in a life after death. As the Divine is manifested through the things of this world and expressed through secular forms, so Inferno is peculiarly rooted in this world and erects its own edifices by means of temporal materials. Certain elements, already present, are intensified, while others are ignored. Because it bears a resemblance to the already existent and familiar, functions with the aid of practices, creeds, and symbols already accepted by many, and is staffed by human beings, peoples are deceived into submitting to the malevolent regime. Inferno has a recognizable government, including familiar titles and procedures, bureaucracy, typewriters, red tape, paper forms, carbons, and directives. Cabinet ministers are appointed, ambassadors dispatched to foreign capitals, and even a parliament may assemble and go through the ritual fragments of its functions.

An institutional drive of this intensity never reaches a stable equilibrium, it is fated to express its nature by an insatiable search for full assurance of its own perpetuation through constant efforts at further expansion and the find-

ing of new areas and enemies to conquer. Where the bar-
baric means employed are aimed at a future good, the
drive will contaminate and cause the course of development
to deviate from the goal into a purely organizational direction, until the movement is a prisoner of its own methods.
Whatever the original proposals for a transformed community
might have been, in the case of Russian Communism the
political organs served chiefly as instruments on behalf of
the institutional drive. So obsessed with an increment of
power was the movement that planned increases in production ostensibly for popular welfare could not then be spared
for this purpose and instead were added directly to state
power. Worthwhile projects that were undertaken invariably
seemed inextricably entangled with the mania to glorify the
regime. (Oswald Spengler's observation that monumental
building is often found in conjunction with the despotism of
a world empire is worthy of note, whatever one may think
of his belief that both mark the decadence of a civilization.)
Nor could the Communist party tolerate the autonomous
presence of any other organizations, either surviving from
the older community or potentially emerging out of the new
ones, since these would limit total control and disperse the
power.

Originating in the requirements of the institutional drive
is an obsessive study of techniques for manipulating both
individual behavior and the operations of all permitted social
organizations in the country. An analysis of the nature of
revolution by a man like Lenin becomes purely a search for
methods whereby power might be seized, regardless of the
will or welfare of the people. Once in authority, further
techniques are developed whereby the governing group may
continue unquestioned masters of society. So skillfully can
governmental and party strength be deployed that even characteristic historical phenomena, common patterns of histori-

cal sequences, may be reproduced artificially in such a manner as to present a surface appearance of reality and validity. Communist governments have been able to foment violence and anarchy in a pattern, to reproduce, to their own textual satisfaction, the outward appearances of a popular revolution, while a fascist regime could simulate the upsurgence of outraged national feelings against its enemies. Institutions, created for purposes of law and order, culminate thus in a dramatically different function, a perversion wherein government becomes the ultimate end in itself.

A particular version of good and evil necessarily crystallizes out of the complete triumph of a particular institutional drive. Anything which contributes to the welfare of the triumphant cause thereby becomes virtuous, and the act of doing good consists in unwavering obedience to it, while evil, on the contrary, lurks in anything opposed to the object of loyalty. (Thus Goebbels: "Propaganda has only one objective, to conquer the masses. Every means that furthers this aim is good; every means that hinders it is bad.") All other standards, including inherited religious ethics, cease to exercise influence where the *Realpolitik* of the government is involved. Even Hell has its laws, and these are dictated by the organic requirements of the organization.

An object of worship must exist, an ultimate gravity in the scheme of things, the nation, class, or religion, which becomes *the* truth, and to which all necessarily sacrifice their energies and talents, even life itself. In addition, a human symbol, a "saint" who is the incarnation of the crusade, usually fulfills the popular need for a personality cult. Other symbols and rituals, very often formerly used by long established institutions or organizations and capable of evoking deep emotions and loyalty, are employed. The ceremonies are most usually copied from the military, for, by reason of its nature as the ultimate in disciplined social action, the marching of men in uniform and the music of the military band are dear to the hearts of the fanatics of the institutional drive. Through it, the individual becomes a dedicated part of something greater, something with a positive and immediate conviction of direction and mission.

When institutional barbarism becomes the law of the land, the willing servants of Inferno themselves are also reduced to the level of prisoners, forced to behave as devils rather than as human beings, regardless of their own better nature. A special kind of logic exists in Inferno which urges men to go to its level and live there, whether it be the persuasion of false gods or merely the path of least resistance. A person's conduct is determined by the dictates of an organized barbarism, wherein he is forced to actions which he knows are morally wrong, and yet, as an individual, the logic of state impels him to commit them. Even the leaders are powerless to escape the grip of the system without sacrificing their own lives.

Within the community a continuous state of war prevails, in which all persons are considered participants whether the individual wishes to enlist or not, and he must pay the penalty, also, if he chooses the wrong side. As if this were a war against a national enemy, every citizen is mobilized in active support of the cause, and the person who refuses to be so enrolled finds his name automatically listed in an opposition which must be liquidated or rendered harmless. Just as on the battlefield, the sacredness of personality becomes completely irrelevant. For those who will not conform, means are found either to segregate them permanently from society or to re-educate them in concentration or labor camps. In these, the modern system of education and the preparation of people to live in our modern society are reversed — this is deliberate retrogression by every means at the disposal of the regime, the methodical destruction of the modern personality.

Witnessing the emergence of a political Inferno, the citizen of authentic Wonderland can only see in the phenomenon the ingredients of an authentic Inferno, and the peasant caught in the imprisoning grip of this sinister incubus must in time also come to recognize the true nature of the forces aroused in his midst. One who bore the rich and personal faith of a true Christian, one whose intellectual perspective, derived from centuries of the Western Tradition, collides directly with this antagonistic twentieth-century barbarism, would see a deeper parallel. The leader of the mass movement, who *must* deny God in word and act in order to achieve mastery over his people, is recognized as playing an ancient role, that of pretending to be a savior, a Messiah, sent to save the people. He very often appears in whatever guise is most popular in that era and makes his kingdom an Inferno not so much by espousing this particular cause as by elevating it to cosmic proportions, to the utter exclusion of everything else.

For the religious person, the legions of an Antichrist could well seem to have infiltrated Leviathan, disguised themselves as Leviathan, which the multitudes then unknowingly worship. The resultant regime often is a caricature of our own, imitating its lineaments with a horrid faithfulness as though Lucifer, the fallen angel, were rebuilding his realm with the things of this day and age in a camouflage so successful that his kingdom may appear to be a genuine Wonderland. A false truth, complete with symbols, creeds, and dogma, comes into being, oftentimes cast in a shadowy approximation of religion, as if the light were casting its shadow. Even in the guardians of Inferno the religious mood exists, and very often the ideas are couched in language evoking those elements in human nature which respond to religious expression;

being human, they cannot completely lose their spiritual impulses, but they are focussed upon purely temporal purposes. As the incarnation of evil in the medieval sought to corrupt the good and thus to undermine the Christian soul and commonwealth, it now strikes at the modern personality, seeking to restore a former condition of ignorance.

The lords of Inferno, trodding a tangible environment and wielding its energies, assume that they have proven themselves the masters of the *real* world. The men faithful to the Christian tradition could find an explanation clearly enough expressed in an excerpt from Karl Vossler's summation of Dante's Inferno:

> . . . Heaven . . . drives Hell to the last extremity, forces man, bestialized and disintegrated by passion, into consciousness, moulds out of the beast, under the pressure of the most terrific divine grace, a new man: a negative man, a non-man, who no longer sins from weakness, but willfully. This human horror can come into being only if the divine spirit gives him a new clarity and strength of will; that is, gives him clear vision and strength of will to work evil.

> . . . It fancies that it is Hell by its own handiwork and of its own strength. Threateningly it displays its shapes of terror; for it is a question of concealing its own nature, which is helplessness. The man who lets himself be frightened by such images of terror, and beguiled into belief in the real power of Hell, is lost and turns to stone.[1]

Dante describes the innermost regions of the evil realm as being frozen, and the modern Inferno strikingly parallels this condition, for its atmosphere culminates, among its lost souls, in a numbing certainty of the artificiality and emptiness of everything civilized man values, a primeval rejection of their veritable existence. This region is as sterile of humanity, its

[1] Karl Vossler, *Mediaeval Culture: An Introduction to Dante and His Times,* translated by William Cranston Lawton (New York, 1929), Vol. II, p. 250.

language as nonhuman, as the technical jargon of a surgeon or engineer. In erecting a power-generating machine in which the individual is simply a unit of productive energy, the institutional drive has destroyed the vitality of the personality. The husks of human existence survive, but the substance, the quality of humanity is gone, replaced by the sheer impersonal appetite of the organization.

Political Inferno is the end result of the institutional drive when, with the aid of modern tools, the state can penetrate into every facet of society and so, in the totalitarian state, achieve complete consummation. An institutional drive, which in its purest form knows no other law than its own fulfillment, replaces a genuine reign of law and the spirit of civilization by the abuse of sacred symbols and tradition; and in laying hands on the very vitals of that which holds society together and thereby debilitating them, in exploiting the soul as well as the body of its citizens, the state saps all bases for its own existence, except through purely physical coercion. The governmental structure itself becomes artificial, only a material shell of a state and of the once-living materials which normally hold a society together, but which now lose all sense of truth except the sheer verity of existence. This is nothing less than the ultimate residue of government, the end of the process, when this particular element of society — a major one, but nevertheless one of many — goes out of control and devours the other elements.

In some such fashion as this, one must recognize the lineaments of an earthly Inferno to balance the vision of an earthly Wonderland. This kind of Inferno has become a reality of the twentieth century, an incontrovertible fact whose presence becomes as compelling a factor in our thoughts and plans as the evolution of our modern technological system itself. The struggles of civilized man against savage tribes beyond the Great Wall of the frontier have ceased; the pioneer into Wonderland encounters his barbarians *within* the community, as organized groups or as the government finds it expedient to create them. Barbarism, not separated from us by time or space, lurks everlastingly beneath the surface in modern society, and the contemporary community reverts to it whenever circumstances encourage its success. The corollary of existent Wonderland is potential Inferno.

8

GROOVES OF CHANGE

In no period of history have men been borne along as ineluctably by sustained, permeating currents of change as in our age. Often dreading its uncertainties or fearing the wounds sometimes incurred, the citizen simultaneously welcomes its exciting opportunities. Men of this century, so accustomed to the deeply imbedded flux within the community that they continue to consider this normal, have learned to reckon with it in their personal environment far better than they comprehend its workings in the commonwealth as a whole. And yet, on this higher level, we are driven into the future under the compulsion of dire consequences if we fail to adapt to our new frontier.

A man of seventy returning to the town of his childhood will very probably have great difficulty in even recognizing it; over the years its physical appearance is likely to have undergone almost complete transformation, unlike a community in earlier days. Though still located on the same site, the town has nevertheless journeyed, year by year, farther into that new nongeographical terrain gradually opened up by the magic of Wonderland. This new frontier in hitherto unexplored territory, with its creation of new spheres and patterns of human activity, poses an endless succession of perplexing problems and entails a constant process of adjustments for individuals, families, and communities. Where these are not made with sufficient dispatch or intelligence, a price must be paid; the cumulative effect of delay is punishment by inconveniences, frustrations, missed opportunities, or worse. To some extent, every town undergoes perpetual chastisement because its citizens do not appreciate the possibilities or are unable to co-operate for their achievement. Many of the evils in even the most advanced community are the direct consequence of difficulty in adjusting to new circumstances in a Wonderland still in the process of creation.

It has been thus ever since the inception of the Industrial Revolution greatly accelerated the tempo of change. From the very beginning of the chain reaction of inventions, every new discovery that solved one problem immediately begot others, both technical and social. The factory system came into existence in England, obviously an instrument of progress and yet in the absence of regulations also bringing with it a flood of abuses; a society accustomed to conditions of work in the cottage handicrafts could not quickly react to the new realities by public measures of restraint. Even when legislative steps against vicious conditions were instituted, the early statutes lacked teeth or merely nibbled at the edges of the problem, and not until the workers themselves enforced their wishes through organization was this particular series of maladjustments in large part rectified.

The automatic chastisement by natural means for violations of laws of conduct in the new environment is clearly evident in the case of the automobile. Though the physical model soon ceased to resemble a horseless buggy, our attitudes still tend to be oriented about assumptions that antedate the use of the motor. The roads were, and usually still are, thoroughfares designed for the two-way traffic of carriages and wagons moving at relatively uniform speeds. Each successive curtailment of movement, through such devices as the installation of additional stop signals, constitutes a visible punishment for permitting the maladjustment to grow, a piecemeal withdrawal of a privilege originally bestowed on citizens by the technology of Wonderland. In the continued conflict of outmoded concepts against the obvious imperatives of the situation, the casualty lists grow longer than they ever did in the old-fashioned kind of military warfare.

The processes of evolution in Wonderland grind on incessantly, varying from one field to another with multitudinous overlapping and in varying magnitudes, in a continuous pattern of growing maladjustments, attempted palliatives, lesser or greater punishments, and ultimate rectification. On the level of national politics, legislation consists, in part, of a never-ending struggle to catch up with changes that have already occurred in the social and economic spheres of the country. The bulk of the accommodations, of course, occurs on the level of the lesser communities, state or local, or within the associational framework. In a democratic country the question is primarily one of how long maladjustments will be endured, how much the pressures will be allowed to mount before corrective measures are undertaken.

For his own survival, the American pioneer was obliged to master a code of conduct in dealing with nature, the

Indians, and his neighbors. On the new frontier of Wonderland, the imperatives may be more subtle or complex, but the consequences of ignoring them can be even more devastating. Slow and erratic but ultimately inexorable penalties are automatically suffered for failures to conform to new necessities, and the more deeply into Wonderland we penetrate the greater the impact upon us. If tangible realities fail to persuade the direction of remedial action, mounting distress follows until a successful effort is made to alleviate the situation. Mankind thus finds itself forced, often against its own will and inclinations, to complete its entry into Wonderland through the continued coercion of the process whereby the modern community has evolved since its inception.

Gross violations of the natural order of Wonderland may result in the harsher chastisement of a political Inferno. Where changes come too quickly in areas undergoing rapid transition to the modern community, the compounding of fundamental errors is likely to ensue from the hurried and clumsy methods used in achieving the technological revolution, as well as from a one-sided appraisal of the nature of society. A forced growth under political auspices, or drastic, wrenching changes by political decree, may very well violate the true nature of Wonderland so radically as to produce a veritable Inferno on earth.

An organized Inferno, in politics or war, develops out of *many* violations of the nature of the modern community. No one act and no one man is responsible; whether the entire community bears collective guilt or not, this tool of natural punishment metes out rough justice upon a whole people in sweeping erratic blows like those inflicted by nature's storms.

Undoubtedly the single most spectacular example is to be found in twentieth-century warfare: the failure to settle disputes by the methods of Wonderland, the sins of omission and commission which cause wars, and the retention of increasingly obsolete political forms result in an automatic chastisement upon all who must share in the conflict. Trapped in the structure built over the years by the institutional drive of the state, individuals must participate in the struggle and share in a judgment brought upon all in a perfectly natural and logical sequence of events through their own collective action or inaction. In addition to the diversion of a man from some of his most fruitful years and the gamble of his life with the dice of chance, the citizen is punished through the peculiarly appropriate necessity of doing evil while knowing that it is evil. Caught in the iron laws of onrushing events and knowing that submission to the enemy would be a worse fate, he must kill and destroy; in payment for the transgressions of his community, logic compels him, as in the political Inferno, to descend to the level of the barbarian.

Like science itself, war has passed beyond human dimensions into the assumption of powers that man has hitherto regarded as divine. In Goethe's *Faust* the devil is made to say that at least God has not given men control of the thunder. But now man has *taken* this control! In arrogating to ourselves the powers of gods, we have also unwittingly ascended into a domain where we are brought into an ever more taxing struggle with the powers of evil. Wonderland's appallingly stringent laws become constantly more exacting, as technology advances, and, if their compulsions are not obeyed, more terrible in their capacity for vengeance. Every accession of power increases the potential of evil, giving it, in the words of Max Ascoli, "a self-denouncing, all-pervading impact."

One final undoubted Inferno, uniting even bitter enemies in sober awareness of the common destiny of all mankind, has materialized, as the peasant gazes anxiously for the mushroom cloud and wonders if it will rain death upon his green acres. When mankind can go beyond the holocausts of mass murder to the annihilation of life upon the planet, in an ultimate self-imposed judgment that it is not fit to survive, the punishment takes on the qualities of the final apocalypse. The Christian may recall Paul Gustave Doré's illustration for the Book of Revelation wherein the people are shown taking refuge in caves in order to escape the latter days' fire from the heavens, and he may discern in this ultimate devastation, the suicide of man, the ancient adversary of the divine in man. Antichrist would seem to emerge from his earlier guises in a final and decisive form — the failure and destruction of that experiment in human potentialities incarnated in the never forgotten figure of the Nazarene. Now that the living offspring of the Creation have seized the prerogatives of divinity and boldly confront the universe, Antichrist calls forth against them, in thermonuclear weapons, the utterly unknowing energies — the ultimate inanimateness of space.

II

Manifestly, the holocausts of our century, and the constant threat of even greater ones, reflect gross violations of the nature of emergent Wonderland. Responsible for them, particularly, is that overly intensive institutional drive of the state that has been nourished by the desperate competition among the nations. Those very features which seem to provide safety from conquest, centralization and discipline, have become, concurrently, an obstacle to the adjustments required by new circumstances, both within a country and among the peoples of the earth.

In the panorama of history one sees change tending to occur, as it were, in a compartmentalized form. Thus, the Protestant Reformation did not radiate outward through its personal acceptance by individuals as they chose or by an expansion on an even front, it came to power in a seemingly haphazard manner by scattered cities or principalities; regardless of individual inclinations, the machinery of state moved as those at the levers of government determined, whatever motives guided them and whatever confluence of events, coincidences, or accident spurred the action. Furthermore, the ingredients of this movement had long been afloat in Europe, a certain conjunction of circumstances and events finally bringing their coalescence into a major uncontrollable upheaval. A nineteenth-century France did not evolve into a democracy increasingly each year; its politics oscillated back and forth repeatedly before the long-term trend definitely asserted itself. Parliamentary government in Europe in the last century, after encountering prolonged resistance, quickly materialized over a good part of the continent, even in areas not ready for it. A country does not normally achieve independence by gradual steps; it leaps forward into full-fledged political life with breath-taking speed, once intense nationalist activity surmounts crumbling resistance. The collapse of the traditional empires in the years centering about the First World War came with startling suddenness. The undercurrents were there in each case; seen in the long perspective there was evolution, and yet there came the decisive moment, that which G. J. Renier calls "the appointed time," [1] when pent-up pressures achieved their goals.

A historian can sketch a list of factors influencing a given episode of change, a revolution perhaps, and in so doing he depicts the rise or decline of the active social forces which were involved. These broad energies, however, do not exercise their influences directly; it is impossible to imagine a situation where the social forces — economic factors, social pressures, the flow of ideas, and so on — have completely

[1] Gustaaf J. Renier, *History: Its Purpose and Method* (Boston, 1950), pp. 232–233.

free play in the community. They must be expressed through vehicles or power structures of some sort, and by their creation an intermediary element is introduced which, in concentrating these energies and giving them mobility and direction, becomes an integral part of the whole process. Organizations, however, are not passively sensitive tools for the transmission of impulses from the basic forces which give them sustenance. From a purely theoretical point of view, to the degree that their activities distort, diminish, or accentuate the social energies, they are an artificial element intruded into the process.

That is, although not furnishing the underlying pressures for change, the natural functioning of the organizations and the interactions among a number of them play a decisive role in the *timing* of the alternating periods of stability and years of flux. The institutional drive of these organizations, while providing the concentrated dynamic of movement, also interferes with the theoretically natural flow of history, of the processes of continuity and change, as these would normally be expected to manifest themselves out of the economic and social forces of the community. Even if the nonpolitical growth within the community occurred at an even rate (which it does not), this evenness would not be reflected in the tempo of political action because the unpredictable confluence of factors and institutional drives implicit in the interaction among *many* groups results in the spasmodic pattern typical of historical evolution.

A compartmentalization of the community energies is produced by the normal growth of associations, and the momentum of the drives then accentuate these divisions. Powerful groups continue to push into positions stronger than their intrinsic functions would proportionately warrant, until, finally, the exigencies of institutional security dictate a secure formalization of enhanced status, an *entrenchment* of position by legislation in order that it may be permanent. In a changing community whose quality is of the temporary and transitional, the successful organization, trying to carry its momentum of success into the future, labors for stability and continuity.

The stronger the institutional drive and the closer its claims approach to the absolutist, the more will an organization thwart or distort the natural processes of change. Because the national state possesses potentially the strongest of institutional drives, it illustrates most starkly the imperfect competency of all organizations as social tools in this process. It remains the prototype of the all-inclusive association which pretends to total representation of all its members. Even when viewed through its own definition and its own assumptions, however, the national state has often been an awkward vehicle for the forces of the age, inasmuch as neat divisions of geographic territory susceptible to clean-cut delineations of frontiers along ethnic lines have always been the exception. Beyond the nationalist criterion, the claims of a national government to speak for all of its people collectively is a dubious proposition in view of the many diverse groups, a heterogeneous collection of many goals and practices, encompassed within its borders. Each group, including others than racial and religious, has its circumstances defined by whatever balance of power may prevail in that community, an arbitrary and rigid prison which may confine it by the accident of proximity and subordinate it to agencies essentially alien to its own nature. The ultimate outrage and patent absurdity caused by the imposition of the national state as dogma, rather than as a social tool, occurs in the forced emigration of folk from areas inhabited for many generations merely because they happen to belong to a different language group.

To a degree unavoidable by the sheer necessity of co-ordination for social action, an intensive drive will nevertheless stifle the multiple variant foci of energy in the country. It is not a question of the worthwhileness of the national state as the primary nexus for all social groups — or the utility of any lesser organizations which to a smaller degree have the same effect — merely an urgency in stressing that, beyond a certain level, the more intensive the drive, the less satisfactorily does it function within the context of the ever-changing energies of Wonderland. Though the national state has become the major vehicle for implementing formal changes, its *overweening* role is not necessarily the most salutary for community welfare.

As the most completely entrenched of all organizations, the state is likely to be far more rigid than nonpolitical organizations. Instinctively throwing its weight on the side of permanence, it alone retains the right, legally, to use violence in preventing change. The refusal of the old-fashioned national state to revise boundary lines or alter the status of any other form of national property without employing force constitutes conduct in diametric contrast to the flexibility demanded by the conditions of Wonderland. Had the associations maintained a similarly obdurate rigidity, neither the government of Wonderland nor the continuation of its material development would have been possible.

The national state inherited from its predecessors a mode of conduct long dominant, and still too evident in some areas, which as a political tool makes it seem a relic of politics prior to Wonderland. Under static conditions or the typical slow-moving circumstances of most of history, the crude, blunt political instruments fitted societies which made a virtue of living according to the ways of their forefathers. In the context of the present, however, the national state often illustrates the limitations of most historical organizations of the past when they were confronted by conditions of multiplicity and change.

Even under modern conditions it may, functioning as a dictatorship, prolong stability in the community indefinitely, if prepared to resort to the most brutal methods of institutional barbarism and if able to retain the loyalty of its armed forces. The ultimate explosion, when the government falters, is likely to be the greater; that is, the degree of violent change, when it comes, is roughly proportional, one may suspect, to the degree of exaggeration of the institutional drive. A despotic regime may be followed by genuine revolution, a phenomenon of modern history made possible by the ability to create organizations on a popular basis, which then offer a practical alternative outside the framework of existent governmental institutions. Lacking the conservative momentum of habitual practices and goaded by fear to rapid entrenchment, the new organizations will probably push changes to a radical extreme, the whole process as damaging a violation of the natural community as was the preceding era of suppression.

The contrast between the politics of the old order and of Wonderland parallels, very broadly speaking, the difference in the theories of the nature of the physical universe in the last century and in this one. During the nineteenth century, with rapidly improving but still comparatively slow means of transportation, it was natural to think of political compartments in terms of territorial segments within which the economy and its people could operate under a single set of regulations. Distances, the age-old obstacle, were being conquered and the citizens were so aware of the victory that areas of land became the axiomatic political base, the unit of political life being thought of as an absolute territorial space bounded by a legally infrangible periphery. An increasingly literate populace, coming alive politically, found their natural demarcation lines quite naturally in the limits to which their language extended. The concept of the non-

divisible political entity, the unified national state in a world
of such states, corresponded well with the physics of the
nineteenth century, wherein the units of the physical world
were also regarded as solids.

During the present century, however, this concept has given
way to a scientific visualization of the universe, again broadly
speaking, in terms of foci of energy from whence radiate forces
having no precise terminal limitations; nature's twentieth-
century image now provides the better model for the infinitely
complex phenomena of society. With distances so mastered
that they are less meaningful, the basic configurations are to
to be found in the nonpolitical nuclei of will and their channelized patterns for exercising power that have been brought
into being by, and are dependent upon, the social and economic forces in the community. These nuclei, foci of individual interests, are of all sizes and qualities, and their
energies radiate outward in different ways and without specific limits.

In a purely geographic sense, also, the energies of Wonderland remold the scene in their own image. The pattern which
emerged in America, where the forces had relative freedom
from political obstructions, has been one of great metropolitan
areas serving as the nuclei for the economic life of the country, and from them the lines of communications and transportation radiate outward into the countryside. Within each
of these regions, sometimes spreading over several states,
are numerous lesser nuclei, smaller cities, which serve their
immediate surroundings. A highway map conveys a visual
image of the pulsating organism that is Wonderland; if the
highways were also designated according to the volume of
traffic by varying thicknesses of lines, the diagram would
be even more precise. This is a map of the genuine Wonderland, a striking example of the forces at work within — and
bursting beyond — the political blocks of land. Within a larger

country, new natural interrelationships are created that run athwart the older territorial jurisdictions, while at the same time these influences would, where free, sweep across national frontiers. The emphasis shifts from the boundary line to the forces that oftentimes would breach that barrier. If one were to superimpose a transportation map of Europe for, say, 1935, upon its 1935 political counterpart, the tyranny of the nationalist institutional drive becomes particularly obvious.

To the degree that the associational system gains ascendancy over and uses territorial representation, a politics has emerged which reflects more accurately, though still crudely, the energies flowing from the multitudinous nuclei, economic or otherwise, in Wonderland. However well adapted, compared to older regimes, it inevitably works in a rather wooden fashion because the fundamental attribute of modern society lies in its basic *forces,* the energies arising out of individual and group needs, rather than in *forms,* the organizations, which serve as the vehicles for these energies. Even at best, the system constitutes an imperfect and insensitive mechanism for registering the needs of Wonderland. Necessary as these vehicles may be as a practical device, the triumph of this political pattern in Wonderland must draw attention to their basic defect, the innate tendency to intensify their institutional drives, thereby accentuating the artificial elements and reducing the ease and relative painlessness of natural change. The healthy community is characterized by the prevalence of associational drives strong enough to restrain changes of a precipitate nature and yet not sufficiently powerful to be able to block imperative alterations.

III

Thus, during the twentieth century, the forces of Wonderland, nourished within the protective confines of the sovereign national state, have begun to burst the frustrating barriers of the nation and to reshape world politics in accordance with their own image. Though mankind was, in the words of the poet, the heir of all the ages, and in the foremost files of time, it could by no means speedily cope, on this scale, with the ringing grooves of change. The natural punishment came in two great world wars.

On the battlefields of the First World War the weapons of emergent Wonderland had rendered obsolete the military textbooks of the generals. Nevertheless, the mass assaults across open ground, men's unprotected bodies against steel, continued, for no alternative could be rapidly improvised, or more truthfully, the commanders could not bring themselves to adopt revolutionary changes quickly enough. Men were fighting not only the human enemy, but, even more, the impasse created by their own inventions. They were prisoners of their own habits, clinging to the usage of military forms and tactics no longer suitable for the forces in their possession.

Nations bearing the energies of emergent Wonderland marched to war as though they were Stone Age villagers going out to throw rocks and primitive spears at one another. Men of all callings, bound in amazing discipline by the ties of the nation, filed into the trenches of death, an abattoir created by historical currents seemingly too powerful for humanity to control; political forms unadapted to physical energies of this magnitude brought about a holocaust partaking less of man-made destruction than of blind nature's destructions. Statesmen, as futile before the new forces as the generals, postured and made their decisions within the framework of the European state system, its untrammeled sovereign nations and diplomatic balance of power.

The forces of Wonderland have been confronting the West, since early in this century, with maladjustments on the international level as bewildering as those the West had earlier brought to the rest of the world when it overwhelmed countless tribes and drove the more advanced countries into a radically altered development. As though introduced from another planet, the burgeoning forces of Wonderland were setting up intolerable tensions in the existent structure and imposing imperative requirements beyond any immediate capacity for a successful response. The penalty for failure was the return to armed conflict in the late 1930's, a planetary civil war in the guise of another war among nations.

In the course of this new military ordeal, Wonderland created, for its own defence, a new weapon based on atomic energy. In so doing, it did more, for in a paradoxical way, Wonderland was drawing out of its own authentic and peculiar genius protection against its own destruction. Technology, by making the waging of war increasingly self-destructive, would abolish it; here lay a decisive and in time inevitable solution to the dilemma of the age. Wonderland's existence would remain in jeopardy until the obsolescence of military warfare among nations became so manifest that its burdens were thrown off, but, unless all rationality had vanished, the armor-plated dinosaurs, so often locked in lethal conflict, were now destined to disappear in a changing political climate.

The total inability of the small states to withstand attack during the Second World War also destroyed the physical reality of old-fashioned sovereignty, while the obvious weaknesses of the national unit in terms of economic self-sufficiency underlined the dependency of the nation upon a larger international community. To the extent that the political state continued to base its actions upon the assumptions of complete sovereignty, it was struggling vainly to maintain the morality of another day and to enforce principles which, decade by decade, were losing validity.

Under the duress of thermonuclear weapons and ballistic missiles, the final unanswerable compulsion has been added to the continuing transformation of the system of sovereign states into a planetary community of free peoples. Adequate channels of communications and negotiations would have to be found and fitting political tools grow out of pragmatically developing practices, either in or alongside the United Nations. The international community had become more than a paper charter or a debating society, however ineffective its institutions might seem when compared to the authority of the state. Regardless of its imperfect performance, the pressing needs of the economy and the horror of the military alternative were forcing the nations to resort to them and, astonishingly, to find in them an escape from their own loudly proclaimed pretensions. Over the years, the practices in the Assembly of the United Nations had assumed some of the characteristics of a parliament, the nations, for instance, forming pressure blocs among themselves in order to gain advantages in the voting. In a manner similar to that of a national parliament, the transactions completed were the product of negotiations and agreements reached outside of the debating chamber, and the compromises reached, good or bad, bore a distinct resemblance to the crude justice achieved by genuine legislatures. As countries were forced to employ other forms of rivalry than the military, their actions increasingly assumed characteristics like those of the major associations within the national community.

The European national state had emerged in the stress and

uncertainty of an age of growth, change, and multiplicity; the necessary reign of a wider law, order, and obedience was galvanized in the hitherto provincial mind through the guise of the nation. It was a political and cultural instrument carrying a sense of equilibrium for the individual in a time of change. And yet this same transformation of society marched swiftly onward until in the perspective of Wonderland the nations quickly became an anachronistic anomaly. Though many of these countries possessed fewer citizens than there are residents in the areas visible from the Empire State Building, any one of these could isolate itself and erect legal walls across the radiating highways of Wonderland. Unlike the populace of a New York City or a Chicago, its citizens could surround themselves with a quality of complete separateness and invest themselves with an independent collective personality.

Within the community of Wonderland one of these would constitute a large association, but the mystic quality of nationality conferred upon the united citizenry a spirit of absolute possessiveness over souls and bodies. The nation-state could impose total authority over each member and set for him, in his brief years of life upon this planet, the path he must follow and the adventures he must confront. It, alone, had the legal power willfully to snuff out the light of consciousness in multitudes of human minds. The railroad lines, telegraph wires, and concrete highways in turn crept over the landscape as Wonderland grew, but still the collective personality, like some atavistic spirit out of the tribal past, could inspire its members to hate and fear the strangers in the valley across the pass. In its proportionate capacity to mobilize power, in the ability to channelize energies for its own purposes, the nation became the greatest of all associations. As conceived by extremists, or as it assumes a totalitarian form, it is an association which has run wild — greatly assisted by inherent qualities and political patterns inherited from its political predecessors.

Military functions of the state obviously have served as a major determinative in the precise shaping of modern government. Nothing has spurred the excessive manifestation of its institutional drive as much as the chronic conditions of war, immediate past, present, or impending future. The competitive international order compels a nation to achieve the greatest possible strength in land, resources, population, and strategic sites, forces it to grow more or less constantly in power and in control over its citizenry; fears of attack generate an incessant compulsion, an unanswerable argument, in persuading citizens to accede to increasing controls.

Now in the process of realization, emergent out of the intrinsic nature of Wonderland, is the obvious solution to this dilemma. The nation organized as a state is, after all, also an association, the strongest, but nevertheless sharing in the characteristics and tendencies of other social organizations. In the same way that the major associations have been increasingly tamed within the framework of democratic government, so the state need no longer generate an absolutist institutional drive as it achieves security within a genuine community of nations.

A permanent cessation of national armed conflict would initiate a series of changes as revolutionary as any in an already revolutionary era. At first maintaining their postures, partly out of incredulity that genuine peace had actually been attained and partly out of institutional inertia, the massive power structures would then begin to respond to the changing circumstances as some pressures declined and others assumed a greater proportionate importance.

If military requirements no longer enforced country-wide discipline, the centripetal forces of the community would be weakened, and the centrifugal drives proportionately assume ascendancy, as the long trend toward a stronger central government would gradually be reversed. One may recall the nineteenth-century conflicts between the two tendencies wherein the centripetal pressures were almost invariably victorious. Thus, the victory of the Union in the United States, the defeat of the Sonderbund in Switzerland, the creation of a unitary government in Italy, and the failure of Communard or regional movements in France and Spain proved the ideal of small autonomous republics within a confederation to be an illusory vision. Modern revolutions, started in the name of liberty, nevertheless concluded by strengthening the state. One must wonder whether the results would always have been the same had not the long-term consequences of the military factor existed. If the military pressures were to dwindle, the localized minority groups throughout the world might, in time, be permitted genuine autonomy within the larger national framework. Another of the major centralizing factors in democratic countries, the associational recourse to the power and wealth of the state, would, of course, still be operative, though eventually some of these responsibilities would undoubtedly be devolved upon the natural subdivisions created by modern economic progress.

Without entering into any discussion of the financial effects of an end to the staggering costs of armaments and the possibilities opened up by the release of this money for different purposes, a number of other important consequences suggest themselves. For instance, the favorite bulwark of dictatorship vanishes when the strong man can no longer point to national peril in justification of his regime. Nor would recourse to war or threats of war be available as an escape from harassing internal problems. Not that dictatorship would miraculously vanish, but once the ability to unleash international violence is gone, the despot would be at a disadvantage; with his principal weapon, the armed forces, reduced to the size and quality of the Latin American level, the will of an aroused populace against unpopular government could more easily be asserted. In these circumstances, this particular set of emotion-packed shibboleths will lose their effectiveness as despots' tools, thereby helping to disintegrate the tenacious cement of the authoritarian state. Tyranny, stripped of this disguise, is likely to stand exposed as simply — tyranny. The ending of war, furthermore, would close the principal school for training of barbarians and greatly reduce those circumstances which have led to the utilization of institutional barbarism.

Whereas the Marxists once anticipated the withering away of the state as a result of the abolition of capitalism and an end of *class* struggle, mankind might look, with more hope, to the consequences of the abolition of nationalist struggles upon the powers of the state.

The Anglo-Saxon countries were enabled to play their creative role in the evolution of the governance of Wonderland precisely because they had the relative security to permit the venture in freedom's political tools. The metamorphosis of international relationships from forms of violent conflict to those akin to associational rivalries would restore our traditional freedom from excessive government and spread these benefits to the other peoples as well.

As the evolution proceeds, the nation would increasingly assume the character of the largest political association, that is, one of many within a planetary community of territorial groupings, each encompassing the countless lesser associations within itself. In learning to accommodate itself to the presence of others, the use of violence, removed as a right from individuals long ago and subsequently also taken away from associations, will cease to be of utility to the nation except as a police measure. The last absolutist element in society would enter a period of profound metamorphosis as Wonderland's proliferation of associations is extended and consummated with the assumption of genuine associational characteristics by the greatest of organizations.

Were the withdrawal of the military factor in the state to be as prodigious in its effect as here surmised, the consequent evolution would see a partial dismantling of the structure of the central government. Some functions would be devolved in a regional direction, while others were assumed by supranational institutions along the lines of those in Western Europe. Still other services might be supervised by relatively autonomous nonpolitical authorities and by associational means. Such a dispersal of power, by endangering the position of the state as the fulcrum in the balance of power among organizations, unquestionably could, in the long run, open up the way for excessive associational aggrandizement, unless the equilibrium retained its full vitality. Nevertheless, the more immediate effect would probably be a renewed plasticity, enabling the inherent forces of Wonderland to mold the shapes of the community in accordance with their own requirements.

Over a century ago, when the tools of Wonderland were just beginning to be contrived, the poet had dipped into the future to see a Vision of the wonder that would be. And the wonder, during a hundred years of emerging Wonderland had come, the magic sails, the ghastly dew from airy navies grappling in the skies. A parliament of man was in session, and the common sense of most sought to hold fretful realms in awe.

The war drums have not yet ceased to throb, but it is past time for the battle flags to be furled — the drumbeats of the marching battalions have ceased to be the pulse beats of civilization. As the plot of history forever changes, the sport of war has faded into the past with the duel of swordsmen and the charge of cavalry, and now the chapter is closed; no longer can the standards of the peoples plunge through the thunderstorm of battle. Its name would now be planetary cataclysm.

IV

From the beginning, America's destiny has been to be a promise of the future, a province of emergent Wonderland; it never was a national state in the narrow European sense, and, pulsating with the energies of Wonderland, it has become a living society transcending that of the nation. When drawn into international politics, the Americans brought a sweeping difference in approach. Without experience in the reasons for the creation of strongly centralized states, or militarism, or the balance of power, they long remained naive and obtuse about these historical phenomena. Finding one mode of expression in the surviving Calvinist spirit, the Americans fought battles for righteousness and were prone to discern the devil and his works in their enemies. They sought total victory, the obliteration of the evil, rather than following the former European custom of partial conquests; the latter demanded relatively minor transfers of land, while the Americans asked no territory but insisted on the *conversion* of their antagonists.

Another spirit besides Calvinism was at work here, however, the mood of Wonderland itself, impatient of obstructions, instinctively seeking to sweep away the inherited social forms and practices which were impeding the progress of the new order. Americans could only see either useless and old-fashioned survivals of the past or, if they were more dangerous, a diabolic apparition which must be destroyed. The American, the peasant migrant with experience of other lands also, lived in more than just another territorial unit among other units, and his perspective was greater than merely national. He represented a transformed society which had evolved out of the old, and could not understand why other peoples should hesitate to join the cause of his new Wonderland, the obvious land of the future.

Implicit in the American attitude ever since the founding of our novel and astonishingly successful republic in a world of monarchies has been the assumption that we represented the coming future against the old-fashioned relics of an evil past. Though ostensibly taking our place as a national state in a society of similar nations, our vision was continental. Imperial in our ultimate territorial domain, our twentieth-century dreams were nevertheless not of expansion; they were, rather, that our kind of normal society should increasingly be duplicated in the other countries of the world. Far from claiming to fight national wars against enemy states, we have consistently interpreted our recent conflicts in terms of a defence of our way of life among other peoples also.

Our Wilsonian dispensation, after the first great war, visualized a world community of free nations leagued together by the common interests of the Elect against potential evildoers. This initial response to the international dilemma of the age could not be effectively implemented, due to the natural persistence of organizational habits of the past. The nationalist pattern of the nineteenth century reasserted itself, although, with the passage of the years, the pressures of Wonderland continued to mount, thereby rendering increasingly frustrating the arbitrary subjugation of the economic and technological energies to the requirements of the international chess board. This deep-seated maladjustment could be sensed in the forcedness and shrillness which made the diplomacy of the thirties seem a rather grotesque caricature of the nineteenth century; there was, in fact, a subtle shift in emphasis, the appearance of the characteristics of rebellion against authority, tentative at first, and then more flagrant as initial success emboldened the rebels.

A political vacuum not yet filled by authority prevailed within a planetary society of peoples just in the process of becoming a veritable community in its own right. Much time and experience would be required for Wonderland's own mode of political conduct to replace the habitual responses, and the resultant vacuum tempted the dissidents to action. Under the traditional European polity, the old-fashioned balance of power among armed nations would speedily have blocked further expansion, but the revolutionary changes of the past decades had vitiated its true vitality, if not its attitudes of mind. The international scene rather resembled the internal situation in some countries during the transition to Wonderland; that is, the new constructive forces were not yet prepared to activate the necessary new authority. Groups which refused to accept the new rules held the initial advantage; civilized man lost the opening battles with institutional barbarism, as he frequently does in the initial onslaught of the barbarian.

The Hitlerian movement rose at least partly as a rebellion, as a secession from the emerging world community by those Germans who felt most keenly the catastrophe whereby Germany had suddenly lost its presumed prewar leadership. For them, the amorphous cluster of allied nations was merely an alliance of victors against the defeated and which hypocritically masqueraded under moral principles. In the very violence of their resistance, however, rested an implicit admission of the intrinsic strength of the new international community; though still only a shadowy presence, the emergence of a new authority stimulated insurrection against it, a dramatic testimony to its reality despite the lack of adequate institutional powers. When this authority failed to assert itself, the rebels, Germans and others, became increasingly insolent and derisive. Heard over the short wave radio, the sound of a Nazi mass meeting conveyed an uncannily accurate portrait of the movement, the noises of the cheering crowd sounding like the howling of a slavering mad beast. Hatred, jealousy, fear, the evil side of man disciplined into the organized murderous system of an Inferno, had been driven into an Opposition to the emergent international community of free nations in Wonderland. Nevertheless, it possessed no stature of its own, was not a legitimate Opposition; like the fiends of Dante's Inferno, the enemy had been brought into being by creative forces, by a constructive evolution which isolated and drove into rabid action those who disagreed.

Though the United States failed to recognize its own ordained role during this period, it was fated, in time, to shoulder its new Manifest Destiny, the leadership among its colleagues, by reason of size and power. To it, eventually, fell the principal responsibility for both the protection and progress of Wonderland as its advance generated centers of opposition.

After the Second World War such an Opposition once again asserted itself, partly as a continuation of the earlier Communist struggle against "Capitalism" and partly generated by the overwhelming attraction of Wonderland. Communism could not engage in free competition with the West for the minds of mankind, since its own peoples would obviously have speedily abandoned their own camp. In order to survive at all, it was compelled to barricade itself behind an Iron Curtain of isolation, censorship, propaganda, and police, while any effective competition required the mobilization of its resources, the stinting of material well-being, and a concentration on the weapons and strategy of the rivalry. Where possible, it aped Wonderland, a grotesque performance when silhouetted against the Inferno of its Stalinist politics.

Perhaps the claim of the Communists that the Western

Powers were aggressive was not entirely chicanery in their mouths. To them, the West must have seemed aggressive, as Western ideas, seeping in despite all their efforts, permeated the air of the despotic states. An intangible pressure incessantly emanated from the midst of their own people; the enduring witness that their conditions no longer were necessary, forced the regime, for survival, to the tightened grip of the institutional drive. If Wonderland were not so successful, Inferno would not be so evil — might not even be an Inferno!

In the last analysis, the overt issues of the era were not the basic ones. Though the Second World War may have been fought out as a conflict among nations, its meaning went deeper than this, nor could the subsequent Cold War be precisely identified in terms of Capitalism versus Communism. The basic struggle lay between the pluralistic and the totalitarian communities, whose would-be oligarchies are the custodians of the intense institutional drive. Fundamentally, the whole process consists in the taming or destruction by the modern planetary community of those institutional drives which have gone out of control and thereby imperil the continuing advance of Wonderland. Stated in a different form — mankind is struggling to escape the crusades on behalf of false earth gods in which it has been entrapped in our century.

Possibly the greater dimensions into which we are entering will be persuasive of altered attitudes. If the magnitude of thermonuclear energies enforces an end to warfare, perhaps also, as man learns to travel in space, his planet will be seen physically in a perspective mankind already knows through higher religion, and the earth gods, postulated by the bearers of the institutional drive, correspondingly lose their compelling attraction. Into the first few fearful glances of the astronaut is compressed a wisdom millenniums in the learning on earth. Amidst the immensity of Space, where conscious life is a total alien, the fact of a material universe, the womb in which our spirits have been borne, would be of less consequence in its texture and contours than the sacredness of the life created within it.

From this perspective, the panorama of history on this planet assumes an orientation vastly different from the dogmatic assumptions of most of mankind. Those domains and institutions which have bulked so large on the historical scene, those organizations which have imposed controls over large masses of humanity, viewed across the long distances of History might well remind one of clouds seen from Space. They are ephemeral hosts of human beings, gathering and dissolving as they are subjected to a gravity created by their own numbers and driven to and fro by the currents in their own vicinity. Nature's clouds, however, are not in themselves an ultimate function of Earth, since it evolved a higher form of life capable of ordering its behavior. The clouds nourish, even if at times they may wreak destruction; but the green fields of the peasant and his work have now, since man the created has assumed the role of creator, become the basic reason for the existence of these energies. Similarly, the social organizations and institutions, with the increasing autonomy of the many-faceted personality in their midst, no longer furnish the final goals of human endeavor. Even as nature's forces are increasingly subjected to specific purposes of a community, so the social energies must be adapted to the specific needs of the individual as he tills his garden.

In the valleys of Wonderland the former peasant has seen the seeds take root and grow. His to determine, as never before, are the contents and productivity of the rich acres. Politically and socially, he cultivates no longer with wooden plow and oxen, and he harvests not with sickle, though the weeds of evil must forever be hacked out. His fields ordered and controlled by eternal vigilance, lest they relapse into wilderness, he now looks speculatively into the heavens and contemplates another odyssey of the human spirit.

INDEX